Henry Mullish is a widely recognized author of calculator books and teaches at New York University.

Richard Kestenbaum, an adjunct professor of international business at New York University, received his MBA from Harvard Business School and is a partner in the merchant banking firm of R.S. Ehrlich & Co.

Financial Analysis by Calculator

PROBLEM-SOLVING TECHNIQUES WITH APPLICATIONS

Henry Mullish and Richard Kestenbaum

Richard Balkin, General Editor

A SPECTRUM BOOK

PRENTICE-HALL, INC., Englewood Cliffs, New Jersey 07632

Library of Congress Cataloging in Publication Data

MULLISH, HENRY.
Financial analysis by calculator.

"A Spectrum Book."
Includes index.
1. Calculating-machines. 2. Calculating-machines—Problems, exercises, etc. 3. Business mathematics. 4. Business mathematics—Problems, exercises, etc. I. Kestenbaum, Richard. II. Title.
HF5688.M83 332'.028'53 82-524
ISBN 0-13-316018-1 AACR2
ISBN 0-13-316000-9 (pbk.)

A SPECTRUM BOOK. Printed in the United States of America.

10 9 8 7 6 5 4 3 2 1

Editorial/production supervision and interior design by Carol Smith
Cover design by Jeannette Jacobs
Manufacturing buyer: Barbara A. Frick

ISBN 0-13-316018-1

ISBN 0-13-316000-9 {PBK.}

PRENTICE-HALL INTERNATIONAL, INC., *London*
PRENTICE-HALL OF AUSTRALIA PTY. LIMITED, *Sydney*
PRENTICE-HALL CANADA INC., *Toronto*
PRENTICE-HALL OF INDIA PRIVATE LIMITED, *New Delhi*
PRENTICE-HALL OF JAPAN, INC., *Tokyo*
PRENTICE-HALL OF SOUTHEAST ASIA PTE. LTD., *Singapore*
WHITEHALL BOOKS LIMITED, *Wellington, New Zealand*

FOR GLORIA

Contents

Preface

This book is intended to guide you through the basic concepts of modern finance. The book builds on itself, beginning with the most fundamental concept—time value of money—and extends through more developed calculations such as annuities, break-even analysis, foreign currency, ratio analysis of performance, and depreciation. It concludes with a discussion of the most prominent theories currently under study in the financial world and includes examples of investment opportunities. We have written it to be of direct practical use to the student of finance, the accountant, the storekeeper, the businessperson, the broker, and the financial analyst—in fact, anyone faced with the task of coping with financial problems.

The broad scope of the book ensures that no matter what field of specialization you may be in, there will be something of interest for you, be it a clearer explanation of a business concept, a specific financial problem, a simpler approach to an otherwise difficult concept, a better method of arriving at a solution, or an explanation of how to exploit the modern financial calculator.

Gone are the days when arriving at a solution to a problem meant hours or even days of arduous, nerve-wracking calculations. The modern calculator assures you of almost instantaneous results on the basis of which decisions may be made immediately.

All that is required on your part is a careful reading of what we have included in the book. We assume that you possess (or have access to) a calculator; the experience of actually running through a problem yourself is the best possible teacher. We have selected for demonstration purposes two of the most popular financial calculators on the market: the Hewlett-Packard HP-38E or HP-38C and the Texas Instruments MBA, which illustrate the two different kinds of logic used in most modern pocket calculators. Even though these two calculators are excellent machines it is not essential for you to own either of them to derive benefit from reading the book. If you have any calculator of your own, you will find the book useful, since the problems, methods, and examples described here can easily be adapted to most machines. If you own a financial calculator, so much the better.

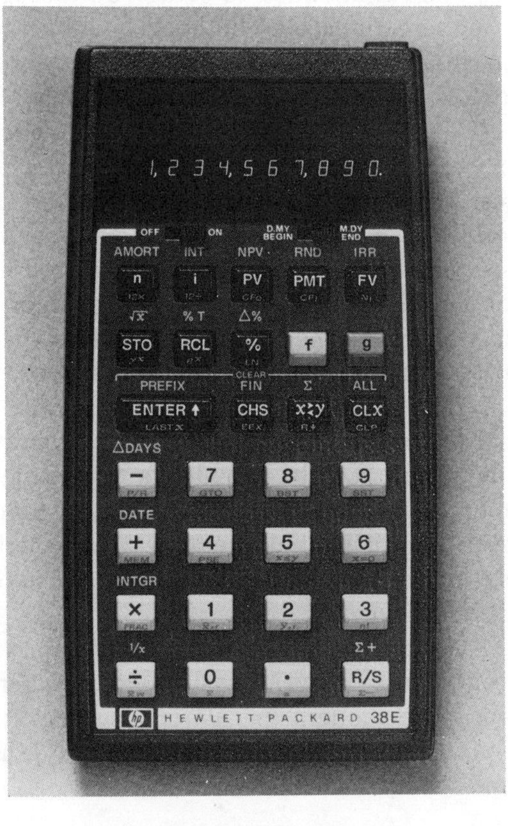

Courtesy of Hewlett-Packard Company

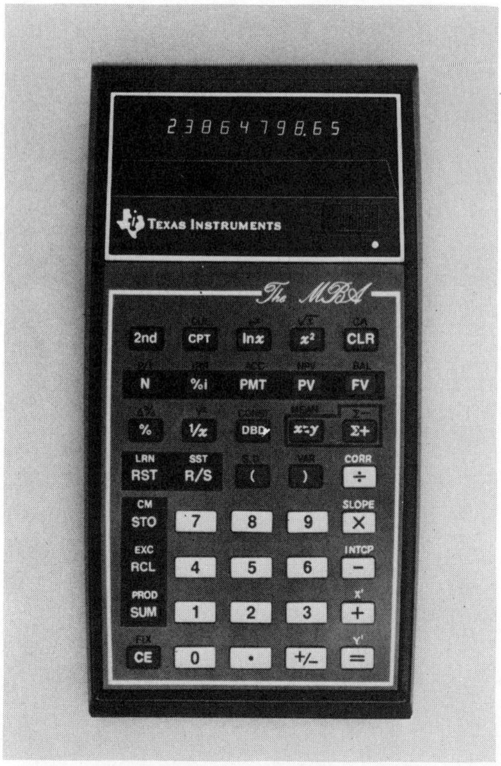

Courtesy of Texas Instruments Incorporated

A novel inclusion in the book are case studies that illustrate many of the concepts described in the text. Moreover, the cases demonstrate the need for human judgment in finance. In the cases there is no single correct answer. Rather, the reader must exercise personal judgment and gather all the support for a decision that can be mustered from the facts of the case.

The case method used follows the style and format advocated by the Graduate School of Business Administration of Harvard University. Consequently, the book is ideally suited to serve not only as a leisurely introduction to the basic concepts of finance but also as a supplementary textbook for an introductory course in finance.

Financial Analysis by Calculator

1 The Pocket Calculator

HISTORY AND DEVELOPMENT

Not until 1971 did the pocket calculator as we know it today come into being. This remarkable tool, with a "brain" composed of literally thousands of electronic components crowded onto a sliver of silicon, is a direct result of the miniaturization of electronic components necessitated by the requirements of the Space Age.

Before 1971 the world had to content itself with bulky, noisy, and cumbersome electromechanical desk-top calculating machines, which not only were slow in arriving at a result but also broke down far too frequently. These machines, which operated to the rhythm of *ka-chung, ka-chung, ka-chung* (when they worked) became known as *Ka-chungers.* It is no wonder that when the first electronic four-function pocket calculator became available in 1971, at the price of about $400, it was received with unprecedented enthusiasm. It is worth noting that in the year 1971 no fewer than one million of these silent machines were sold in the United States alone. Overnight, the *Ka-chunger* became obsolete and was shipped off to the museum.

Since that time the price of the ordinary four-function calculator has fallen so fast that it can now be bought for well under $10. In the interim we have witnessed the remarkable growth of specialized calculators, including those specifically designed for the financial community. Parallel to this growth has been the development of the programmable pocket calculator, which provides the consumer with the advantages of a computer compressed into a model so compact it can slip unnoticed into a shirt pocket.

As the keyboards of the HP-38E or the TI-MBA clearly show, the number of functions available at the touch of a key has grown by leaps and bounds. These functions include square root, reciprocals, x^2, the trigonometric functions—sine, cosine, tangent, and their inverses—logarithmic functions and statistical functions, in addition to memory cells in which intermediate results can be stored for later recall. Another feature that is meeting ready acceptance is the continuous-memory calculator, which stores a keyed-in program as well as individual results, even though the calculator may be switched off. The HP-38C is, in fact, the continuous-memory updated version of the 38E, to which we make frequent reference throughout this book.

CALCULATOR LOGIC

When pocket calculators first became available, calculations were performed in a strict sequential manner. That is to say, a calculation of the form

$$2 + 3 \times 4 =$$

was keyed in exactly in the order shown above in a left-to-right direction. The answer given by the calculator was invariably 20. This is the answer that most simple four-function calculators would give today. If you have a calculator nearby, why don't you try it yourself? See if you get 20. Don't panic if you don't; we will shortly explain any discrepancy.

A mathematician looking at the foregoing equation would be tempted to give an answer of 14 rather than 20 because in mathematics there is a rule that within any given arithmetic expression, multiplication precedes addition. Texas Instruments decided to recognize this mathematical hierarchy, and in many of their better calculators they implemented a logic system dubbed Algebraic Operating System (AOS). Under AOS the expression

2 + 3 X 4 =

yields the result 14 because the multiplication of 3 by 4 is done *before* the addition of 2. Texas Instruments's MBA calculator, being an advanced model, operates in AOS. Here are some simple arithmetic instructions performed on the MBA. Before looking at the results, try to arrive at your own conclusion, bearing in mind that in the absence of parentheses, all multiplications and divisions are done first (in a left-to-right order) and all additions and subtractions are done last. If parentheses are present, their contents are evaluated first according to the hierarchy described above. Don't forget, cover up the answers first.

Expression	*Result*
5 + 3	8
7 + 5 X 1	12
3 X 4 + 8	20
8 + 3 X 4	20
8 + 4 X 3	20
4 + 3 X 2 - 1	9
(6 + 2) - (3 + 4)	1
(6 X 2) - (3 + 4)	5
(6 ÷ 2) - (3 + 4)	-4

If you got any of the above calculations incorrect, it would be worthwhile to go over them very carefully to be sure you understand the principles involved. Carrying out those problems on a calculator that does not operate under AOS logic will produce results that will not agree with ours.

All of the Hewlett-Packard pocket calculators, regardless of model, operate in what has come to be known as Reverse Polish Notation (RPN). Even though this may sound esoteric, once you have gotten used to it, it will become second nature and prove to be quite efficient.

Just in case you are wondering why this logic is known as Reverse Polish logic, this is no ethnic or political joke. In 1949 Dr. Jan Lukasiewicz, a Polish mathematician, invented a parentheses-free but unambiguous mathematical language. Over the years it has undergone some development and change and has now become known to us as Reverse Polish Notation in honor of the good doctor. The reason for the word *reverse* is that initially the arithmetic operator (+, −, ×, etc.) was placed before the two numbers (operands). In RPN the operators are placed *after* the operands—the *reverse* of what Dr. Lukasiewicz devised.

All of the calculators manufactured by Hewlett-Packard are wedded to a four-register memory stack, which permits the solving of complex algebraic equations without parentheses or even an = key. All intermediate results are displayed as they are calculated. During the course of calculation they are automatically saved and retrieved as needed.

The essence of RPN is that whenever an operation is to be carried out on two numbers, both numbers must have been keyed into the calculator before the desired operation is specified. In other words, if we want to add 2 and 3 together, we would first key in the number 2 and press the ENTER↑ key to separate it from the 3, which is keyed in next. Only after both numbers have been keyed in is the addition key pressed. At that moment the operation is performed and the result, 5, appears in the display. Notice that under RPN there is no equal sign, since there is never a need for it. All results, intermediate or otherwise, are automatically sent to the display. Since there is no hierarchy of operations involved, the order in which operations are performed is at the discretion of the user. For example, the expression

2 + 3 × 4 =

may be keyed into the HP-38 either as

2 ↑ 3 + 4 ×

(where the upward pointing arrow denotes the ENTER↑ key) in which case the expression is treated as if it were written

(2 + 3) × 4

This yields a result of 20. However, it may be keyed in as:

3 ↑ 4 X 2 +

in which case the expression is evaluated as if it were written

2 + (3 X 4)

which yields the result of 14.

Let us now consider the expression

(6 + 7 − 8) ÷ 20

This would be keyed in as:

6 ↑ 7 + 8 − 20 ÷

giving a result of 0.25. On the other hand, the expression

20 ÷ (6 + 7 − 8)

is keyed in as

20 ↑ 6 ↑ 7 + 8 − ÷

giving the result of 4.00. Notice in this case that to keep the numerator of 20 separated from the denominator—which had to be evaluated first—the ENTER↑ key is pressed twice during the calculation and the division held off until the very end.

Here are some typical arithmetic expressions. The keystrokes required to evaluate them are shown to their right. Remember, the upward pointing arrow indicates that the ENTER↑ key is to be pressed.

Arithmetic Expression	*RPN Keystrokes*	*Result*
2 + 3	2 ↑ 3 +	5
(3 X 4.6) − 8	3 ↑ 4.6 X 8 −	5.80
7(5 + 19 − 14)	7 ↑ 5 ↑ 19 + 14 − X	70
(18/2) X (17 + 3)	18 ↑ 2 ÷ 17 ↑ 3 + X	180

SELF-TEST PROBLEMS

Try to solve all of the following arithmetic expressions using your calculator—whatever model you have. You should arrive at the same result regardless. Once you have written down all your calculated results compare them with ours, which you'll find in the appendix at the end of the text.

Arithmetic Expression

1. 7 + 2 - 6
2. 4 × 3 - 5
3. 8(5 + 3)
4. 7/14 - 9
5. (13 - 6) × 8
6. 13 - (6 × 8)
7. 5 - (2 × 3) + 3
8. 9/3 + (6 + 2 × 3)/3
9. 9/3 + 6 + (2 × 3)/3
10. 9/(3 + 6) + 2 × 3/3
11. (2 + 3)/10 × 3
12. 2 + 3/(10 × 3)

Manufacturers of calculators using RPN and AOS each claim that their method parallels the way one normally thinks. However, few people will argue the fact that RPN does require some getting used to. But once it has been mastered, calculations can be done swiftly and with a high degree of confidence. Some argue so strongly in favor of RPN that they would refuse to handle a calculator that did not use that form of logic. Conversely, many others feel the same way about AOS.

The controversy over whether RPN or AOS is the better system will probably never be resolved. Actually, it is a question both of personal preference and the particular kinds of problems one normally encounters. Either form of logic is perfectly suitable for the kinds of financial problems in this book.

2 Time Is Money

If you had the good fortune to possess $100,000 you would essentially have two choices before you concerning how to use the money. You may choose either to spend it or to save it. Should you choose to spend it you could probably buy something like a new home or several choice automobiles, or treat yourself to a trip around the world. If, instead, you chose to save it you would probably do so with the expectation of accumulating an even greater sum.

SIMPLE INTEREST

One method of saving is the conventional savings account at the local savings bank. These institutions effectively borrow money from you and other depositors and pay you "rent" (in the form of interest) for the privilege of borrowing your money, in much the same way as a tenant pays rent to a landlord for the use of the landlord's property.

Most interest rates are quoted in annual terms; that is, if you left the money invested for a period of one full year the amount of interest you would receive would be the annual rate quoted to you by the bank. If, for example, the savings bank in which you deposited your $100,000 paid 5.75 percent interest annually, after one year you would have a total of

$105,750. Here is how we may arrive at this figure using the two calculators.

HP-38

Step	*Key in*	*Display shows*
1	100000	100,000.
2	CHS	-100,000.
3	PV	-100,000.00
4	5.75	5.75
5	i	5.75
6	1	1
7	n	1.00
8	FV	105,750.00

Answer: $105,750

First, the HP-38 calculator is instructed that, in effect, $100,000 is to be paid out by the investor. This is done by keying in the number 100,000 preceded by a minus sign, indicating a negative movement of cash (from your pocket to the bank's coffers). The CHange-Sign key (CHS) converts a number in the display to its opposite sign before pressing the Present Value key (PV). Next the annual rate of interest, 5.75, is keyed in, followed immediately by the i key. As mentioned, the period of time our $100,000 is to be invested is one year, so the number 1 is pressed, succeeded by the key marked n, denoting that the number of years for the life of the investment is one. Now that the three values have been entered into the calculator the machine is ready to compute the future value of our account balance. Since any interest calculations require three values to be entered, the HP-38 "knows" that the fourth financial function key pressed indicates the result desired by the user. Now that three values are in the financial registers of the calculator, to find the Future Value you need only press the FV key. Notice that the displayed future value of 105,750.00 is a positive quantity, indicating a positive flow going from the bank to the investor.

TI-MBA

Step	*Key in*	*Display shows*
1	100000	100000
2	PV	100000
3	5.75	5.75

Step	*Key in*	*Display shows*
4	%i	5.75
5	1	1
6	N	1
7	CPT	1
8	FV	105750

Answer: $105,750

In the above schematic for the TI-MBA, the calculator was first informed that the amount being deposited was $100,000. This was done with the PV key where PV stands for Present Value. Next, the annual rate of 5.75 percent was keyed in followed by pressing the %i key, which informs the calculator that the annual interest rate is 5.75 percent. Since the money is being invested for one year the number 1 is keyed in and the N key depressed, signifying that the Number of years is one. In any interest calculation three pieces of information are always necessary for the calculator to yield a result. The versatility of the calculator allows the user to key in these three values in any order. We picked the order PV, %i, and N quite arbitrarily. We could just as easily have selected the order %i, N, and PV or even N, PV, %i.

Once all the values are entered the calculator is instructed to compute the value of our account balance at a future date—in this case, at the end of one year. Consequently, the keys CPT and FV are pressed, instructing the calculator to ComPuTe the Future Value of our account balance.

COMPOUND INTEREST

In the above example we assumed that the interest was paid at the end of the *year*. This is generally spoken of as *simple interest*. Suppose instead that each month's interest was paid at the end of that *month*, still using the nominal interest rate of 5.75 percent annually. In such a case the bank would have to calculate the rate of interest to be paid at the end of each month. At an annual rate of 5.75 percent the monthly rate would be 5.75 ÷ 12, or 0.48 percent. However, as we shall soon see, the interest paid at the end of the month is paid not only on the original $100,000 but also on the interest accumulated during the previous months. This has the happy effect of increasing the yield to the depositor by *compounding* the impact of the interest payments. Therefore, this has become known as *compound interest.*

HP-38

Step	*Key in*	*Display shows*
1	100000	100,000.
2	CHS	–100,000.
3	PV	–100,000.00
4	5.75	5.75
5	g	5.75
6	12÷	0.48
7	12	12.
8	n	12.00
9	FV	105,903.98

Answer: $105,903.98

As in the previous problem of simple interest, the $100,000 investment is entered as a negative number into the PV register. Since interest is to be paid monthly the 5.75 percent interest must be entered as a monthly rate. The HP-38 provides a unique and useful feature to accomplish this task. The annual rate of 5.75 is keyed in and the blue g key followed by the i key with 12 ÷ written in blue on its lower surface are pressed. A double purpose is then served, in that the 5.75 is divided by 12 and the resulting number (0.48) is *automatically* entered into the i register. Since interest is to be paid *monthly*, the number of months, 12, is entered into the n register. It is worth emphasizing that the time period of the rate of interest *must* coincide with that of the number of periods. In other words, if interest is quoted on a *monthly* basis the number of *months* must be entered for n. If interest is quoted on a *yearly* basis the number of *years* must be entered in the n register.

The future value is obtained by pressing the FV key, displaying the amount of $105,903.98, an increase of over $150 above that yielded by simple interest. This illustrates the benefit to the investor (and, of course, the additional cost to the bank) of compound interest.

TI-MBA

Step	*Key in*	*Display shows*
1	100000	100000
2	PV	100000.
3	5.75	5.75
4	÷	5.75
5	12	12
6	=	0.479166667
7	%i	0.479166667
8	12	12
9	N	12.
10	CPT	12.
11	FV	105903.9832

Answer: $105,903.98

On the TI-MBA to compute the future value of $100,000 invested at 5.75 percent compounded monthly, again the principal amount of $100,000 is keyed in and entered as PV. Since the interest is to be paid monthly the *monthly interest rate* must be determined. This is done simply by dividing the annual interest rate, 5.75, by the number of periods over which it is to be paid, 12. The result, 0.48 (approximately), appears on the screen, allowing the user to enter it as the interest rate merely by pressing the %i key. Since the interest is to be paid over 12 months the number 12 is entered as the Number of interest-bearing periods, via the N key. Pressing the CPT and FV keys in sequence causes the result of 105,903.9832 to appear in the display.

In recent years it has become widely accepted for banks to pay interest not only on an annual or monthly basis but compounded on a *daily* basis. This is even more to the advantage of the investor, as you will see from the next illustration.

Assume that our $100,000 is invested in a savings account at 5.75 percent, compounded daily. Here are the calculations.

HP-38

Step	*Key in*	*Display shows*
1	100000	100,000
2	CHS	−100,000

Step	*Key in*	*Display shows*
3	PV	–100,000.00
4	5.75	5.75
5	↑	5.75
6	360	360.
7	÷	0.02
8	i	0.02
9	360	360.
10	n	360.00
11	FV	105,918.04

Answer: $105,918.04

TI-MBA

Step	*Key in*	*Display shows*
1	100000	100000
2	PV	100000.
3	5.75	5.75
4	÷	5.75
5	360	360
6	=	0.015972222
7	%i	0.015972222
8	360	360
9	N	360.
10	CPT	360.
11	FV	105918.0404

Answer: $105,918.04

It is customary in banking circles to use the number 360 as the number of days in a year. It is for this reason that the interest rate is divided by 360, and that the number 360 is keyed into the N register. We see from step 11 that the final value is $105,918.04, almost $15.00 more than the yield when the interest was compounded monthly.

On occasion banks try to lure investors by offering them accounts yielding interest compounded not annually, monthly, or even daily, but rather on a *continuous* basis, that is to say, the interest is compounded at every moment. On the face of it this seems like a most attractive proposition. Armed with our calculator we can find out if this is, in fact, so.

Both the HP-38 and the TI-MBA have the capacity to convert the interest a nominal rate would pay to the amount that would be paid if interest were compounded continuously.

The function e^x converts a nominal rate into a continuously compounded one. To use this function the nominal rate of interest must be expressed as a decimal fraction rather than as a percentage. Therefore, the percentage must be divided by 100 before executing the e^x function.

HP-38

Step	*Key in*	*Display shows*
1	5.75	5.75
2	↑	5.75
3	100	100
4	÷	0.06
5	g	0.06
6	e^x	1.06
7	1	1
8	−	0.06
9	100	100.
10	x	5.92
11	i	5.92
12	100000	100,000
13	CHS	−100,000
14	PV	100,000.00
15	1	1.
16	n	1.00
17	FV	105,918.53

Answer: $105,918.53

On the MBA calculator the e^x key is upper case so that it must be preceded by the 2nd key. Once the e^x function is calculated, the number 1 must be subtracted from the result. To turn this result into a form in which it can be used for a financial calculation it must be multiplied by 100. From this point on the calculation may proceed in the ordinary manner.

TI-MBA

Step	*Key in*	*Display shows*
1	5.75	5.75
2	÷	5.75
3	100	100
4	=	0.0575
5	2nd	0.0575
6	e^x	1.059185271
7	−	1.059185271
8	1	1
9	=	0.059185271
10	x	0.059185271
11	100	100

Step	*Key in*	*Display shows*
12	=	5.91852707
13	%i	5.91852707
14	1	1
15	N	1.
16	100000	100000
17	PV	100000.
18	2nd	100000.
19	FV	105918.5271

Answer: $105,918.53

The calculators have thus revealed that the advantage of continuous compounding over the course of a year is worth $15 more than a daily compounding on a principal of $100,000.

We have already pointed out that on both the HP-38 and the TI-MBA calculators, given any three of the four values PV, FV, i, and n, the fourth value can be found at the touch of a key. Now we'll illustrate the benefits of such flexibility.

Example 1 A person decides that to retire in 15 years he would like to have the sum of $500,000 in his bank account, which pays 8 percent compounded annually. How much must he deposit immediately to realize his goal?

FV = $500,000
i = 8 percent
n = 15 years
PV = ?

HP-38

Step	*Key in*	*Display shows*
1	15	15.
2	n	15.00
3	8	8
4	i	8.00
5	500,000	500,000.
6	FV	500,000.
7	PV	–157,620.85

Answer: $157,620.85

TI-MBA

Step	*Key in*	*Display shows*
1	15	15
2	N	15
3	8	8

Step	*Key in*	*Display shows*
4	%i	8.
5	500000	500000
6	FV	500000.
7	CPT	500000.
8	PV	157620.8525

Answer: $157,620.85

Example 2 An employee has saved $10,000. He wants it to grow to $50,000 in 30 years. What interest rate would be needed?

PV = $10,000
FV = $50,000
n = 30 years
i = ?

HP-38

Step	*Key in*	*Display shows*
1	10000	10,000.
2	CHS	–10,000.
3	PV	–10,000.00
4	50000	50,000.00
5	FV	50,000.00
6	30	30
7	n	30.00
8	i	5.51

Answer: 5.51 percent

TI-MBA

Step	*Key in*	*Display shows*
1	10000	10000
2	PV	10000.
3	50000	50000
4	FV	50000.
5	30	30
6	N	30.
7	CPT	30.
8	%i	5.51130635

Answer: 5.51 percent

Example 3 How many years would it take for the sum of $500 to amass into $1000 at a 9 percent annual rate compounded monthly?

PV = \$500
FV = \$1000
i = 9 ÷ 12 = 0.75
n = ?

HP-38

Step	*Key in*	*Display shows*
1	9	9.
2	↑	9.00
3	12	12.
4	÷	0.75
5	i	0.75
6	1000	1,000.
7	FV	1,000.00
8	500	500.
9	CHS	–500
10	PV	–500.00
11	n	92.77
12	12	12
13	÷	7.73

Answer: 7.73 years

TI-MBA

Step	*Key in*	*Display shows*
1	9	9
2	÷	9.
3	12	12
4	=	0.75
5	%i	0.75
6	1000	1000
7	FV	1000.
8	500	500
9	PV	500.
10	CPT	500.
11	N	92.76576586
12	÷	92.76576586
13	12	12
14	=	7.730480489

Answer: 7.73 years

Note that since the interest was entered on a monthly basis the answer is correspondingly given in months. To convert to years simply divide by 12.

SELF-TEST PROBLEMS

1. A woman invests $100 at 8 percent compounded daily for five years. How much does she have at the end of the five-year period?

2. The sum of $4500 is invested at 7.75 percent interest compounded semiannually. What will it be worth in eight and a half years?

3. What rate of interest would be necessary for $12,000 to become $18,000 if it were invested in an account that is compounded monthly for a period of three and a half years?

4. How long would it take for a sum of $120,000 to increase to $200,000 if it were invested at 8.75 percent compounded annually?

5. A person is approached with the opportunity to invest in one of two propositions.

Proposition A: Invest $100,000 at 7.50 percent interest compounded daily for ten years.

Proposition B: Invest $100,000 at 6.75 percent interest compounded continuously over the same ten-year period.

Which one yields the greater return?

CASE STUDY: THE GLEEDA ICE CREAM CORPORATION

The Gleeda Ice Cream Corporation is the ninth largest manufacturer and distributor of ice cream in Canada. The company's business is extremely cyclical in that all sales occur during the months of June, July, and August. Accordingly, the company receives a large influx of cash during the warm months, which far exceeds the company's expenses for that period of time. However, to compensate its management staff and maintain its machinery in working order. Gleeda has the following expenses during its less active months:

September	$45,000
October	$25,000
November	$25,000
December	$25,000
January	$25,000
February	$25,000
March	$65,000
April	$45,000
May	$45,000

In March of each year the company starts up its manufacturing operations for the coming summer, which accounts for the bulge of expenses in that month. Similarly, since operations have already commenced in April and May, expenses for those months are substantially higher than in the months during which the machinery is lying idle.

At the end of August the company possesses a large amount of cash, which it uses to cover its expenses in the coming winter months. Historically, Gleeda has always kept its funds in a non-interest-bearing checking account at the local branch of the Grosvenor Trust Company.

Gloria Stieglitz, Gleeda's treasurer, has a reputation for coming up with solid ideas. In the middle of August 1982 she projected that on September 30 of that year the company would have $350,000 in cash on hand. Dissatisfied with the fact that the company would not receive any interest on its money, Gloria contacted a number of other banks to determine what interest rate they would pay to attract Gleeda's accounts. She obtained the following results:

1. Student Bank N.A. agreed to pay 9 percent interest per year, compounded annually, if the money remained on deposit for a period of five years or longer.
2. Ardsleigh Bank offered Gleeda 8 percent interest per year, compounded quarterly. Ardsleigh Bank placed no

restrictions on the amount of time the money had to remain on deposit.

3. Beresford Bank responded to Gloria's inquiry with an offer to pay 8 percent interest per year, compounded daily. However, Beresford insisted that the money remain on deposit for at least six months.
4. Wilson Bank offered to pay 8.25 percent interest, compounded monthly, with the proviso that the money remain on deposit for a period of three months.

Gloria calculated the effective annual interest rate that the various banks had offered and drew up the following table for presentation to the president of Gleeda.

Bank	*Effective Annual Interest Rate (%)*	*Restrictions*
Student	9	minimum period five years
Ardsleigh	8.243	none
Beresford	8.328	six months
Wilson	8.569	three months

Armed with the table Gloria strolled briskly into the office of Shea Gitz, the president of Gleeda Ice Cream Corporation. Shea was not too busy that morning and offered Gloria a seat. They discussed briefly the current status of some operations problems the company was experiencing and at the end of that discussion Gloria said: "I have to admit to you, Shea, that I didn't really come to talk about operations but rather to show you a new idea I have about meeting our winter expenses." Shea leaned forward in his chair. Gloria got up and immediately began to pace the room.

"We've been doing business with Grosvenor Trust for many years. We've always kept a large cash balance in our checking account without receiving any interest on it. I propose that we move our deposits to one of the following banks."

Gloria then produced the table shown. Shea was intrigued. He picked up his telephone and dialed Anthony Chin, vice-president of Gleeda. Shea invited Anthony to join him and Gloria to discuss Gloria's new idea. Anthony entered the office and listened carefully to Gloria's proposal. After hearing Gloria out Anthony responded, "Of course, it's great to draw interest where we were drawing none before. The question is, in which bank do we invest the money? We can't put any money in a bank that imposes restrictions on withdrawal since we'll need the money before we're allowed to withdraw it."

"Just a minute," Gloria shot back. "We don't need *all* the money in the next six months or even in the next three months so we can put *some* of the money in restricted accounts and the money we need right away in unrestricted accounts."

Shea was disturbed. "Let's not forget," he said, "that three years ago we didn't have the money we needed to meet the winter expenses. Because we were steady depositors at Grosvenor they lent us the money to tide us over. I'm not sure it would be wise to sever our relationship with them totally."

Alternative Solutions We are about to present alternative solutions to the Gleeda Ice Cream case. Keep in mind though that none of these alternatives is necessarily the best solution. It is entirely reasonable that you may arrive at a solution with which you will feel infinitely more comfortable. Moreover, the number of possible solutions is limited only by your imagination. Our objective in describing possible solutions is merely to get you started. This holds true for all the cases in this text.

The decision as to which bank Gleeda should deposit its money into rests on both qualitative and quantitative considerations. The quantitative segment has two components:

1. the effective annual interest rate
2. the minimum amount of time the money must remain on deposit.

If Gleeda were concerned with just the first factor then clearly the corporation would deposit all its money with Student Bank N.A., since they pay the highest interest. If the company were concerned only with the second factor then it would deposit all of its funds in Ardsleigh Bank, because Arsleigh imposes no minimum time requirements.

At this point it might seem that the only choices to be considered are Student Bank and Ardsleigh Bank. However, it is possible that one of the other two banks might offer a happy medium of the two extremes represented by Student Bank and Ardsleigh Bank. Indeed, a close scrutiny of Wilson Bank's policy reveals that it pays more interest than Ardsleigh but has a longer deposit time and that it pays less interest than Student but has a less restrictive minimum deposit time requirement. On the other hand, Beresford Bank pays less interest and has more restrictions than Wilson Bank, so it is difficult to imagine circumstances under which anyone with the opportunity to deposit money in Wilson Bank would ever want to deposit money in Beresford Bank.

We propose to deposit Gleeda's surplus funds in portions to be divided among Student Bank, Ardsleigh Bank, and Wilson Bank. This solution will obtain the highest possible interest rate, given that Gleeda seeks to pay its expenses as noted in the case. The amount to be deposited in Ardsleigh Bank should be sufficient to allow the company to withdraw $25,000 in each of the months October through December. The amount to be deposited in Wilson Bank should be sufficient for Gleeda to withdraw the cost of its expenses for the months January through May. The remaining funds not needed for the payment of expenses should be deposited in Student Bank, where they will earn the highest possible interest.

The above solution considers the quantitative issues and arrives at a recommendation that works out best on economic factors. A good manager, however knows that after all the numbers are "crunched" the decision-making process just begins. At that point the qualitative issues must be considered. Over the years Gleeda has established such a relationship with Grosvenor Trust that Grosvenor was willing to lend the company money when it was needed. If Gleeda believes that it will need to borrow money again and that none of the three new banks would be willing to extend credit, the corporation should strongly consider remaining with Grosvenor despite the obvious disadvantages to such a strategy. On the other hand, if Gleeda's relationship with Grosvenor were entirely professional, the other banks should be just as willing as Grosvenor was to lend the money. Only a good manager can assess the relative merits of each alternative and arrive at the proper decision.

What would you do?

3 Annuities

It is easy to imagine the day you are strolling by the local Rolls-Royce dealer and a particular model in the showroom strikes your fancy. In a rare moment of indulgence you find yourself utterly unable to resist the temptation to become the proud owner of that elegant automobile. Upon making inquiries you learn that the retail price of the vehicle is around $50,000, a sizable sum by any standard. You have only $20,000 available in cash but the dealer informs you that the local bank will loan you the balance of $30,000 at 9.50 percent interest to be repaid over a period of four years. The first thought that comes to your mind is how much each monthly payment will be. If it is within reason you will go ahead and make the purchase. Armed with a financial calculator you are fully equipped to handle the situation on the spot.

This type of loan falls under the general category of *annuities*, in other words, it is a financial problem dealing with a series of payments made at regular intervals. We come across many examples of annuities in our everyday dealings. If your home has a mortgage, that is an annuity, as are insurance premiums and the interest you receive on bonds you own. Annuities may take several different forms. First is the case where you make equal payments at regular intervals and receive a large payout at the end of the life of the annuity. If you have ever joined a Christmas or Chanukah Club you will be familiar with such an arrangement.

Second is an annuity in which you pay out a large sum of money at the beginning and then receive many smaller sums throughout the life of the annuity. An example would be the trust fund that wealthy parents might leave for their children in the event of their deaths.

A corporate bond is another type of annuity. A corporate bond, for say $1000, represents the buyer's agreement to pay a lump sum of $1000 to purchase the bond, for which the bond issuer agrees to pay a certain sum of money as interest each year for the life of the bond. At the bond's maturity the company stops paying interest and returns the $1000. A corporate bond is therefore an annuity with the distinction of having a large payment at the end. This end payment is usually referred to as a "balloon" payment.

ORDINARY ANNUITIES

In an ordinary annuity, such as a car loan, payments are made at the end of every period, usually at the end of every month. Returning to our Rolls-Royce scenario, we will now show how the amount of the payment of the annuity can be determined quickly by your financial calculator. As before, the calculator needs to "know" three pieces of information to determine the fourth. In the Rolls-Royce example we know that the present value of the loan is $30,000, the interest on the loan is 9.50 percent per year (or 0.79 percent per month), and that the loan will be outstanding for four years (or 48 months). All that is necessary now is to enter this data into the calculator and have the machine compute the value of the payment (abbreviated PMT).

PV = $30,000
i = 95 ÷ 12 = 0.79 percent
n = 48 months
PMT = ?

HP-38

Step	*Key in*	*Display shows*
1	30000	30,000.
2	PV	30,000.00

Step	*Key in*	*Display shows*
3	9.5	9.5
4	g	9.5
5	12÷	0.79
6	48	48.
7	n	48.00
8	PMT	−753.69

Answer: $753.69

TI-MBA

Step	*Key in*	*Display shows*
1	30000	30000
2	PV	30000.
3	9.5	9.5
4	÷	9.5
5	12	12
6	=	0.791666667
7	%i	0.791666667
8	48	48
9	N	48.
10	CPT	48.
11	PMT	753.6940965

Answer: $753.69

From the above schematics it is clear that the monthly payment is $753.69. Of course, on the HP-38 the final figure is displayed as a negative number indicating that it is to be paid out.

For the next problem we shall compute n given the values of PV, i, and PMT.

Example 1 Suppose a person wishes to put $10,000 into a savings account paying 7.75 percent so that he may draw the sum of $200 per month until there is no more money left in the account. How long will it take to exhaust the account?

Ordinarily the difficulty in such a problem lies in the fact that interest is paid only on the amount still in the account and not on the monies that have already been withdrawn. Your financial calculator, however, is geared to cope with this problem, so you do not have to concern yourself about it at all.

PV = $10,000
i = 7.75 ÷ 12 = 0.65 percent
PMT = $200 per month
n = ?

HP-38

Step	*Key in*	*Display shows*
1	10000	10,000
2	CHS	–10,000.
3	PV	–10,000.00
4	7.75	7.75
5	g	7.75
6	12÷	0.65
7	200	200.
8	PMT	200.00
9	n	60.58

Answer: 61 months

TI-MBA

Step	*Key in*	*Display shows*
1	10000	10000
2	PV	10000.
3	7.75	7.75
4	÷	7.75
5	12	12
6	=	0.645833333
7	%i	0.645833333
8	200	200
9	PMT	200.
10	CPT	200
11	N	60.57581738

Answer: 61 months

For the next problem we shall calculate the value of i given PMT, FV, and n.

Example 2 An investor wants to squirrel away $1000 a year for five years so that she may have a total sum of $6000 at the end of that period. What interest rate must she seek?

PMT = $1000 per year
FV = $6000
n = 5 years
i = ?

HP-38

Step	*Key in*	*Display shows*
1	1000	1,000.
2	CHS	–1,000.
3	PMT	–1,000.00
4	5	5.
5	n	5.00
6	6000	6,000.

Step	Key in	Display shows
7	FV	6,000.00
8	i	9.13

Answer: 9.13 percent

TI-MBA

Step	Key in	Display shows
1	1000	1000
2	PMT	1000.
3	5	5
4	N	5.
5	6000	6000
6	PV	6000.
7	CPT	6000.
8	%i	9.128062317

Answer: 9.13 percent

Example 3 An investor wants to deposit a certain sum in his savings account, which pays 7.8 percent interest, so that he may withdraw $3000 per year for five years. How much must be deposited to permit him to do it?

i = 7.8 percent
PMT = $3,000 per year
n = 5 years
PV = ?

HP-38

Step	Key in	Display shows
1	7.8	7.8
2	i	7.80
3	3000	3,000.
4	CHS	−3,000.
5	PMT	−3,000.00
6	5	5.
7	n	5.00
8	PV	12,041.54

Answer: $12,041.54

TI-MBA

Step	Key in	Display shows
1	7.8	7.8
2	%i	7.8
3	3000	3000
4	PMT	3000.
5	5	5
6	N	5.

Step	*Key in*	*Display shows*
7	CPT	5.
8	PV	12041.53637

Answer: $12,041.54

Thus we see that to withdraw $3000 a year for each of five years from an account paying 7.8 percent interest, it is necessary to deposit an initial sum of $12,041.54.

The value of $12,041.54 is known as the *discounted cash flow* of five $3000 payments to be made over the period of five years.

Example 4 The local bank advertises a Christmas/Chanukah Club in which the depositor deposits $35 per week into an account paying 9 percent per year compounded weekly for the one-year life of the account. What will be the balance (accrued amount) at the end of the year?

PMT = $35 per week
i = 9 percent compounded weekly
n = 52 weeks
FV = ?

HP-38

Step	*Key in*	*Display shows*
1	35	35.
2	CHS	–35.
3	PMT	–35.00
4	9	9.
5	↑	9.00
6	52	52.
7	÷	0.17
8	i	0.17
9	52	52.
10	n	52.00
11	FV	1,902.69

Answer: $1,902.69

TI-MBA

Step	*Key in*	*Display shows*
1	35	35
2	PMT	35.
3	9	9
4	÷	9
5	52	52
6	=	0.173076928
7	%i	0.173076928

Step	Key in	Display shows
8	52	52
9	N	52.
10	CPT	52.
11	PV	1902.692003

Answer: $1,902.69

ANNUITIES DUE

In all of the above examples of annuities we assumed that each installment, and the final payment for that matter, would be made at the end of each payment period, be it a week, a month, a year, or whatever. That is one of the conditions of an ordinary annuity. There is, however, another kind of annuity in which all payments are made at the *beginning* of the period rather than at the *end*. Such an annuity is referred to as an *annuity due*. Most financial calculators are sufficiently versatile to deal with an annuity due. On the HP-38 there is a switch located in the top right-hand corner labeled BEGIN–END, which permits the user to specify whether the payments are to be made at the beginning of a period or at the end, and hence whether it is an annuity due or an ordinary annuity, respectively. On the TI-MBA annuities due are handled by pressing the DUE function instead of the CPT function.

For an annuity due illustration we shall simply take the data from the previous problem and regard it as an annuity due rather than as an ordinary annuity.

PMT = $35 per week
i = 9 percent compounded weekly
n = 52 weeks
FV = ?

HP-38

Step	Key in	Display shows
1—Move switch to BEGIN		
2	35.	35.
3	CHS	–35.
4	PMT	–35.00
5	9	9.
6	↑	9.00
7	52	52.
8	÷	0.17

Step	Key in	Display shows
9	i	0.17
10	52	52.
11	n	52.00
12	FV	1,905.99

Answer: $1,905.99

TI-MBA

Step	Key in	Display shows
1	35	35
2	PMT	35.
3	9	9
4	÷	9.
5	52	52
6	=	0.173076923
7	%i	0.173076923
8	52	52
9	N	52.
10	2nd	52.
11	DUE	1905.985124

Answer: $1,905.99

Since the payments of an annuity due are all made at the beginning of a period rather than at the end, they are left to accumulate interest over a larger period of time. That larger period of time is equal to the difference between the time of the first payment under an ordinary annuity and the time of the first payment under an annuity due. This accounts for the slightly higher return. Historically speaking, annuities due have not played a major role in the financial world. Most annuities, even at the present time, are ordinary annuities. However, since interest rates in recent years have hit record highs the question of who holds the payment during each of the payment periods is becoming more and more significant. It is likely that annuities due will grow in importance.

BALLOON PAYMENTS

Some annuities require a larger payment for the last installment than for all the other payments. In such cases the final payment is spoken of as a *balloon payment* or *balloon*. To place this concept into perspective consider the following situation:

Example A company wishes to build a new plant and needs to borrow $250,000 to do so. The bank informs the company that they would be happy to lend them the money at 10 percent per year compounded monthly if the company agrees to pay $2,500 per month and a $50,000 balloon payment at the end of the loan. How long is the life of such a loan?

This somewhat complex problem must be broken down into two parts. In fact, to solve it on the MBA you have no choice but to split it into two parts.

PV = $250,000
i = 10 percent per year compounded monthly
PMT = $2,500 per month
FV = $50,000
N = ?

Part One: We can treat this loan as if there were no balloon payment and solve for N in the ordinary way. The result of the calculation will tell us how long it would take to pay off the $250,000 if there were no balloon payment.

Part Two: Turning our attention to the balloon payment of $50,000 we will now determine how many months it would take to pay off a loan equal to the balloon payment and subtract that time period from that obtained in part one.

TI-MBA

Step	*Key in*	*Display shows*
1	250000	250000
2	PV	250000.
3	10	10
4	÷	10.
5	12	12
6	=	0.833333333
7	%i	0.833333333
8	2500	2500
9	PMT	2500.
10	CPT	2500.
11	N	215.90577774
12	STO 0	215.90577774
13	50000	50000
14	PV	50000.
15	CPT	50000.
16	N	21.96962157
17	+/−	−21.96962157
18	+	−21.96962157

Step	*Key in*	*Display shows*
19	RCL 0	215.90577774
20	=	193.9361558

Answer: 193.94 months

Part one is represented by steps 1 through 11. The result is stored in memory location 0 in step 12. Part two is represented by steps 13 through 16, while the remaining steps subtract the result of part two from that of part one, giving a final answer of 193.94 months.

The HP-38 is somewhat better equipped to handle this kind of problem than is the MBA; with it the problem does not have to be broken up.

HP-38

Step	*Key in*	*Display shows*
1	250000	250,000.
2	PV	250,000.00
3	10	10.
4	g	10.
5	12÷	0.83
6	2500	2,500.
7	CHS	–2,500.
8	PMT	2,500.00
9	50000	50,000.
10	CHS	–50,000.
11	FV	–50,000.00
12	n	193.94

Answer: 193.94 months

NET PRESENT VALUE

We have already seen that the value of an annuity at its outset is referred to as its present value (PV). If we were to take the present value of an annuity that pays us a certain dollar value each year (paid at the end of the year) and subtract from the present value the amount required to be invested in the annuity, the result would be the net present value of the annuity. This can be clarified with a simple example.

Suppose we have the opportunity to invest $20,000 in an annuity which returns ten payments of $3,000, each paid at the end of every year. Let us assume that at the same time we also have the option to invest the $20,000 in a savings account that yields 8 percent. For the annuity to appear attractive the return on the annuity must exceed that of the savings account. To compare the two options objectively we have to examine the return from the annuity (10 × \$3,000 = \$30,000) and calculate how much that \$30,000 would be worth at the time the two options are being considered, if it is discounted to the present at the rate of 8 percent, the rate of return offered by the bank. Since the annuity must return something greater than 8 percent, this value is referred to as the *hurdle* rate. The discounting calculation is done as follows.

HP-38

Step	*Key in*	*Display shows*
1	3000	3,000.
2	PMT	3,000.00
3	10	10.
4	n	10.00
5	8	8.
6	i	8.00
7	PV	−20,130.24

Answer: \$20,130.24

TI-MBA

Step	*Key in*	*Display shows*
1	3000	3000
2	PMT	3000.
3	10	10
4	N	10.
5	8	8
6	%i	8.
7	CPT	8.
8	PV	20130.2442

Answer: \$20,130.24

Once the present value is obtained, the cost of the investment, \$20,000, is subtracted and the difference is referred to as the net present value. The fact that the net present value is positive indicates that the return on the investment is greater than the hurdle rate of 8 percent. Investing in the annuity would therefore be more advantageous than putting the money in the bank in this case.

Your financial calculator can determine the net present value of an investment directly. This is particularly useful in a case when the cash flows from the annuity are of different amounts. For example, if for a \$20,000 investment we received

$1,000 the first year, $2,000 for each of the next three years, and $4,000 for each of the remaining years, the net present value can be computed directly. Here is how this investment would be analyzed on the TI-MBA (assuming the discount rate is 8 percent).

Cost of annuity = $20,000
Return in year 1 = $1,000
Return in years 2 through 4 = $2,000
Return in years 5 through 10 = $4,000

TI-MBA

Step	*Key in*	*Display shows*
1	8	8
2	%i	8.
3	20000	20000
4	+/−	−20000
5	PV	−20000.
6	1	1
7	N	1.
8	x ≷ y	0
9	1000	1000
10	2nd	1000
11	NPV	−19074.07407
12	2	2
13	N	2.
14	x ≶ y	1.08
15	2000	2000
16	2nd	2000
17	NPV	−17359.39643
18	3	3
19	N	3.
20	x ≶ y	1.1664
21	2000	2000
22	2nd	2000
23	NPV	−15771.73195
24	4	4
25	N	4.
26	x ≶ y	1.259712
27	2000	2000
28	2nd	2000
29	NPV	−14301.67225
30	5	5
31	N	5.
32	x ≶ y	1.36048896
33	4000	4000
34	2nd	4000
35	NPV	−11579.33946
36	6	6
37	N	6.

Step	*Key in*	*Display shows*
38	x ≶ y	1.469328077
39	4000	4000
40	2nd	4000
41	NPV	–9058.66095
42	7	7
43	N	7.
44	x ≶ y	1.586874323
45	4000	4000
46	2nd	4000
47	NPV	–6724.699369
48	8	8
49	N	8.
50	x ≶ y	1.713824269
51	4000	4000
52	2nd	4000
53	NPV	–4563.623831
54	9	9
55	N	9.
56	x ≶ y	1.850930211
57	4000	4000
58	2nd	4000
59	NPV	–2562.627963
60	10	10
61	N	10.
62	x ≶ y	1.999004627
63	4000	4000
64	2nd	4000
65	NPV	–709.8540111

Answer: –$709.85

To calculate the net present value on the TI-MBA each payment must be entered separately. Before beginning one must enter the discount rate (as done in steps 1 and 2) and the initial investment (preceded by a negative sign to indicate outflow). Each of the payments must then be entered separately and numbered in sequence. Accordingly, the number 1 is pressed and registered as the first payment by pressing the key labeled N. The "x interchange y" key, x ≶ y, is next pressed and the first payment amount keyed in.

The 2nd and NPV keys are then pressed, and the net present value for the cash flows entered so far is calculated. This is done for each of the flows until they are all recorded and the answer appears on the display.

Admittedly, such a problem is somewhat tedious and time consuming but it is a far improvement over having to use pencil and paper! The HP-38 is capable of a much more elegant solution to the same problem.

HP-38

Step	*Key in*	*Display shows*
1	20000	20,000.
2	CHS	−20,000.
3	g	−20,000.
4	CFo	−20,000.00
5	8	8.
6	i	8.00
7	1000	1,000.
8	g	1,000.
9	CFj	1,000.00
10	2000	2,000.
11	g	2,000.
12	CFj	2,000.00
13	3	3.
14	g	3.
15	Nj	3.00
16	4000	4,000.
17	g	4,000
18	CFj	4,000.00
19	6	6.
20	g	6.
21	Nj	6.00
22	f	6.00
23	NPV	−709.85

Answer: −$709.85

On the HP-38 the initial cash flow is entered using the function CFo (signifying cash flow at time zero). All subsequent cash flows are entered via the CFj function key and if there is a series of identical flows, the number in the series is entered with the Nj key. For example, since the last six cash flows were all $4000, that amount was entered into the CFj register and the number 6 into the Nj register for repetition purposes. Once the interest rate (8 percent) is entered the calculator may be instructed to compute the net present value via the NPV function.

In both cases we see that the net present value is negative and therefore reveals that we would be better served by placing our $20,000 in the bank than by investing in the annuity. As a rule, whenever the NPV is negative it signifies a weak opportunity for investment. When it is positive, NPV indicates that the investment is a good opportunity. The higher the NPV the greater the magnitude of the opportunity. When NPV is equal to zero the investment is neither advantageous nor detrimental.

INTERNAL RATE OF RETURN

The rate of return that yields an NPV of zero is spoken of as the *internal rate of return* (IRR). To arrive at the IRR for a series of cash flows on the HP-38, once they have been entered one need only press the IRR function. For the above example the IRR is 7.34 percent. That means that had the bank offered 7.34 percent on its accounts the rational investor should be indifferent to putting money in the savings account or investing in the annuity.

To calculate the IRR on the TI-MBA calculator one must first enter the initial outlay in memory #0. All other cash flows are then entered in memories #1 through #9 and memory #. and # +/–. (Yes, these are really additional memories!) Once the cash flows are in place the IRR key is pressed and the correct answer of 7.34 percent is displayed.

TI-MBA

Step	*Key in*	*Display shows*
1	20000	20000
2	STO 0	20000.
3	1000	1000
4	STO 1	1000.
5	2000	2000
6	STO 2	2000.
7	STO 3	2000.
8	STO 4	2000.
9	4000	4000
10	STO 5	4000.
11	STO 6	4000.
12	STO 7	4000.
13	STO 8	4000.
14	STO 9	4000.
15	STO.	4000.
16	2nd	4000.
17	IRR	7.3433185

Answer: 7.34 percent

The major criticism of the NPV method of evaluating an investment opportunity is that it assumes that the cash flows from the investment are reinvested at the same rate as that of the investment opportunity. Since this is not always true, NPV is not always a reliable yardstick.

BONDS

Both the government and private corporations borrow money from groups of individual investors. The government usually borrows money to offset its deficit, which runs into the billions of dollars. Private corporations often borrow money to finance expansion and other new projects. Such borrowing is usually done by the issuance of bonds and other debt instruments in the capital markets.

A typical corporate bond might be sold for $1000 and have a life of 20 years. For $1000 the investor receives semi-annual interest payments whose amount is determined by the prevailing market forces at the time of the bond's issuance. The amount of the interest payment is also dependent upon the quality of the issuing corporation's credit. In general, the higher the credit rating the lower the interest payment. At the end of the bond's life the investor's $1000 is returned. Effectively, the corporation has rented the investor's money for the life of the bond; the rent is paid in the form of interest. A corporate bond can be thought of as an annuity of interest payments with a balloon payment at the end.

If a bond costs $1000 and pays interest of $50 per year, the yield on the bond is 50 ÷ 1000 = 5 percent.

Often when a bond is issued by a corporation or a municipality it is sold for $1000. During the life of the bond interest is paid. At maturity the investor receives the $1000 and all involved are happy. However, this scenario is sometimes far from the truth. Many bonds have a maturity of some 20 or 30 years. Many investors prefer to see the return of their funds before the term has run its course. Consequently, an after-market for the purchase and sale of bonds before their maturities exists among investors. Although the investor may have paid $1000 for the bond, it is more than likely that in the after-market he or she will receive either more or less than $1000 for the bond. This may be the result of several factors: if the general public's perception of the issuing corporation's credit has deteriorated since the issuance of the bond, the investor is likely to get less than the $1000 paid for the bond. On the other hand, if the corporation's credit has been strengthened since the issuance of the bond, the investor will probably get more than $1000 for the bond. Similarly, if prevailing interest rates have moved down since the bond was purchased, the value of the bond will probably be worth more than $1000. If interest rates have climbed, the bond would be worth less than $1000.

Suppose that interest rates do indeed rise and that the investor who originally purchased a 30-year bond now, after 10 years, wishes to dispose of it in the aftermarket. At the time of the sale in the aftermarket the value of the bond is $925. The purchaser of the bond in the aftermarket has paid $925 for the right to receive interest payments and $1000 at the end of 20 years. In an ordinary yield calculation the investor's return is determined by the interest payments divided by the cost of the bond. This is appropriate where the investor pays $1000 and gets $1000 back at the end of the bond's life. However, in this instance a conventional yield calculation is not applicable, since it ignores the fact that the amount received at the end of the life of the bond ($1000) is greater than the amount paid for the bond ($925). Clearly, we should be able to incorporate the differences between purchase price and amount received at maturity into the yield calculation.

The world of finance has provided us with just such a method in the calculation known as the *yield to maturity* (YTM). It turns out that this seemingly novel calculation is none other than our now-familiar formula for internal rate of return (IRR). As you know, your financial calculator has the ability to solve the problem. The underlying concepts will become clear with a simple problem. All that is required to structure the problem is to view the purchase of a bond as the purchase of a series of cash flows.

Example 1 A 15-year $1000 bond of ABC Company issued in 1972 pays interest of $90 per year (9 percent), payable semiannually on February 1 and August 1. In 1982 the original purchaser of the bond decides she now wishes to sell the bond in the aftermarket. Since interest rates in 1982 are higher than those of 1972, the price of the bond in the aftermarket has fallen to $950. What is the yield to maturity (IRR) of the bond for the purchaser in the aftermarket?

Interest to be received in each of the remaining nine interest periods = \$45
Final payment to be received at maturity = \$1000 + \$45
(final interest payment) = \$1045

HP-38

Step	*Key in*	*Display shows*
1	950	950.
2	CHS	–950.
3	g	–950.
4	CFo	–950.00
5	45	45.
6	g	45.
7	CFj	45.00
8	9	9.
9	g	9.
10	Nj	9.00
11	1045	1,045.
12	g	1,045.
13	CFj	1,045.00
14	f	1,045.00
15	IRR	5.15
16	2	2.
17	X	10.30

Answer: 10.3 percent

Note that after the IRR is calculated it is multiplied by 2 since interest payments in our example are made on a semiannual basis and we wish to know the YTM on an annual basis.

TI-MBA

Step	*Key in*	*Display shows*
1	950	950
2	STO 0	950.
3	45	45
4	STO 1	45.
5	STO 2	45.
6	STO 3	45.
7	STO 4	45.
8	STO 5	45.
9	STO 6	45.
10	STO 7	45.
11	STO 8	45.
12	STO 9	45.
13	1045	1045
14	STO.	1045.
15	2nd	1045.
16	IRR	5.15232137
17	X	5.15232137

Step	Key in	Display shows
18	2	2
19	=	10.30464274

Answer: 10.3 percent

Example 2 A purchaser in the aftermarket buys a $1000 bond with three years remaining until maturity. The bond pays interest of $80 per year, payable semiannually. Since the credit standing of the issuing company has risen since the issuance of the bond, the price paid by the purchaser is $1060. What is the YTM of the bond?

Cash outlay for purchaser of bond in aftermarket = $1060
Interest to be received in each of the remaining five periods = $40
Final payment to be received at maturity = $1000 + $40 (final interest payment) = $1040

HP-38

Step	Key in	Display shows
1	1060	1,060
2	CHS	−1,060.
3	g	−1,060.
4	CFo	−1,060.00
5	40	40.
6	g	40.
7	CFj	40.00
8	5	5.
9	g	5.
10	Nj	5.00
11	1040	1,040.
12	g	1,040.
13	CFj	1,040.00
14	f	1,040.00
15	IRR	2.90
16	2	2.
17	X	5.79

Answer: 5.8 percent

TI-MBA

Step	Key in	Display shows
1	1060	1060
2	STO 0	1060.
3	40	40
4	STO 1	40.
5	STO 2	40.
6	STO 3	40.

Step	Key in	Display shows
7	STO 4	40.
8	STO 5	40.
9	1040	1040
10	STO 6	1040.
11	2nd	1040.
12	IRR	2.89622168
13	X	2.89622168
14	2	2
15	=	5.79244336

Answer: 5.8 percent

PRICING A BOND

Assume a bond is offered to you, one that will pay $1000 at the end of five years. The bond also pays $80 per year, payable semiannually. Other investment opportunities that are available make you decide that you would buy the bond only if it would guarantee at least a return of 8.50 percent. What is the most you should pay for the bond? Your financial calculator to the rescue.

FV = $1000
PMT = $40 each six months
i = 8.50 percent per annum, or 4.25 percent per six months
n = 10 six-month periods

On the TI-MBA calculator the problem is broken down into two parts. First the PV of the $1000 payment to be made in five years is calculated and stored. (See steps 1 through 10). Next, the PV of the interest payments is calculated (see steps 12 through 15) and the two figures are added together (steps 16 through 18).

TI-MBA

Step	Key in	Display shows
1	1000	1000
2	FV	1000
3	4.25	4.25
4	%i	4.25
5	10	10
6	N	10.

Step	*Key in*	*Display shows*
7	CPT	10.
8	PV	659.5373022
9	STO 0	659.5373022
10	0	0
11	FV	0.
12	40	40
13	PMT	40.
14	CPT	40.
15	PV	320.4354803
16	SUM	320.4354803
17	0	320.4354803
18	RCL 0	979.9727925

Answer: $979.97

It is important to note steps 10 and 11 where the FV register is zeroed out to ensure that the value previously placed in the FV register does not interfere with the calculation being performed. On the HP-38 the problem can be solved in one sweep.

HP-38

Step	*Key in*	*Display shows*
1	1000	1,000.
2	FV	1,000.00
3	40	40.
4	PMT	40.00
5	4.25	4.25
6	i	4.25
7	10	10.
8	n	10.00
9	PV	–979.97

Answer: $979.97

The calculators have helped us to determine that the most we should pay for the bond is $979.97.

SELF-TEST PROBLEMS

1. If $80 each month is put into a savings account at 8 percent compounded monthly, how long will it take to accumulate $10,000?

2. If you invest $90 each month for 50 months and you want the final value to be $5000, what rate of interest must you get?

3. How much must be invested for an account paying 9.5 percent compounded annually to return an amount of $500,000 if it is invested for 20 years?

4. What will be the final value of an account paying 5.75 percent compounded monthly if $25 per month is invested for 60 months?

5. What monthly payment would have to be made to an account paying 9.5 percent monthly if you wanted to have $500,000 at the end of 20 months?

6. An investor has the opportunity to invest in two annuities, both of which require an $18,000 investment at the outset. Cash flows from the first annuity are as follows:

Years 1 through 3	$2,000 per year
Years 4 and 5	$5,000 per year
Year 6	$10,000
Year 7	$8,000

Cash flows from the second annuity are:

Year 1	$1,000
Year 2	$2,000
Year 3	$4,000
Years 4 through 6	$8,000
Year 7	$10,000

The investor also has the opportunity to put the $18,000 in the bank at 5.75 percent compounded annually.

Choose among the three alternatives and explain why you made your choice. Be sure to consider the NPV and IRR for each of the three investments.

7. Both ABC Corporation and XYZ Corporation are selling bonds that will pay the investor $1000 in five years. The ABC

Corporation's bond pays $80 per year in interest, in semiannual payments. It sells for $1040. XYZ Corporation's bond pays $40 per year paid semiannually and sells for $960.

Which has the higher YTM?

CASE STUDY: THE SHARP FAMILY

"Sheldon, I don't see why we have to borrow money from the bank when our own money is sitting there in a bank waiting for us to use it."

"Well, Jean," Sheldon replied, "I'm reluctant to use our money since we may need it for an unexpected emergency."

When he was first married, Sheldon was a product manager at Robert Phillips, Inc., an industrial products concern in Terre Haute, Indiana. He had been with the firm for a couple of years after he had graduated from the State University at Oshkosh with an M.B.A. degree. His career at Robert Phillips was proceeding well and he was confident that his future at the firm looked bright.

During the same year that their first child, David, was born he and his wife purchased a modest but comfortable two-bedroom house not far from Sheldon's office in Terre Haute. Although the house was smaller than Jean and Sheldon would have preferred, it was the most they could afford at the time. They took comfort in the fact that the house was suitable for expansion at some later date. Sheldon's annual salary of $33,000 enabled them to live comfortably but not extravagantly.

Some years later Jean took a leave of absence from her job as assistant principal in Public School 107 in Terre Haute since she was due to give birth to a second child. Jean and Sheldon calculated the time had arrived for the long hoped for expansion of their home to accommodate their growing family, and they decided to add another bedroom. After much research Sheldon calculated that the cost of the addition to the house would amount to about $15,000.

During the course of their marriage Jean and Sheldon had accumulated almost $20,000 in savings, which was deposited in a local savings and loan association, earning interest at the rate of 7 percent per year. After talking with their bank manager Sheldon and Jean learned that the bank was willing to loan them the $15,000 necessary for the expansion at 8 percent interest per year. They were faced with selecting one of two alternatives: either withdrawing most of their savings from the bank or taking out the loan.

Jean and Sheldon now spent numerous evenings discussing how to finance the proposed addition to their home. Jean, on the one hand, felt that it was bad policy to borrow money unless there was simply no alternative. She reasoned that since they had more than enough in the bank they should use their savings. "Besides," she often added, "we'll get the money back when we sell the house."

Sheldon, for his part, was not overjoyed with the idea. He wanted to use their savings only in the case of their retirement or disability. Having the money in the bank was a comfort that he was not eager to surrender. Using his pocket calculator he determined that the cost of repaying the bank loan would be $125.47 per month for 20 years. Jean and Sheldon continued to discuss the matter but found it difficult to arrive at a mutually agreeable solution.

Alternative Solutions The issues are, once again, both qualitative and quantitative. In this situation the two issues can be intermingled and considered as a whole.

Sheldon wishes to pay an extra one percent over the interest rate they are receiving on their savings to be sure that the money they have deposited in the bank will be available for emergencies. Jean would prefer to save the additional interest cost and not be concerned about whether emergency funds will be needed in the future.

The Sharps can look at the security issue as an insurance question. If they pay the one percent interest cost, they will be insured against having to search for emergency funds up to $15,000 if it should ever prove necessary. Whether the Sharps take that "insurance" or not depends on the level of risk they wish to assume themselves and the amount they are willing to pay to avoid such risk.

4 Break-Even Analysis

Most entrepreneurs envision that their prospective business ventures have the potential to reach the stars. However, even the most optimistic of entrepreneurs must at some point determine at what level of sales (or volume) the company will break even, in other words, the point at which neither profit nor loss is generated. The break-even point should be the minimum level of business the entrepreneur expects to conduct (since anything less will result in a loss). Therefore, it is always important for the break-even point to be known.

Most businesses have two kinds of costs: (a) *variable costs*, which depend on the number of items being produced and include expenditures for raw materials, direct labor hours, fuel, and so on; and (b) *fixed costs*, such as rent, president's salary, property taxes, and so on. The combination of the two is known as the *total cost*. Let us put these terms into perspective with the following example.

Example A businessman has a prospective venture to manufacture faucets, which he will sell at $10 each. The cost of raw materials and all other variable costs are $6 per faucet. Additionally, the businessman must spend $100,000 per month in fixed costs to keep the plant operational; this includes maintenance, rent, and taxes. What is the break-even point of this venture? How many faucets does he have to sell each month to cover both his fixed and variable costs?

If we subtract the variable cost of the faucets from the selling price, the $4 that remains will be used to offset the fixed costs of $100,000 per month. The break-even question then becomes: How many times must the company generate the $4 to cover the $100,000 of fixed costs? The answer is derived by dividing $100,000 by the $4 contributed by each sale. Since

$$\frac{\$100,000}{4} = 25,000$$

we know that to break even he must sell 25,000 faucets a month. The amount contributed by each sale toward offsetting the firm's fixed costs is referred to as the *contribution margin* (CM). The break-even point is equal to the total fixed costs divided by the contribution margin per unit.

$$\text{Break-even} = \frac{\text{Fixed costs}}{\text{Contribution margin}}$$

Here is how the calculation is done on the HP-38:

Step	*Key in*	*Display shows*
1	100000	100,000.
2	↑	100,000.00
3	4	4.
4	÷	25,000.00

Answer: 25,000 faucets

On the TI-MBA the method is:

Step	*Key in*	*Display shows*
1	100000	100000.
2	÷	100000.
3	4	4.
4	=	25000.

Answer: 25,000 faucets

The concept of contribution margin is an important one in understanding the profitability of a business. ABCD Conglomerate Corporation has four divisions, each of which operates autonomously. The head office of the corporation serves only to advise and consult with the divisions when necessary. Under this arrangement the head office generates expenses without directly producing any revenue, in other words, it is a cost center. Consequently, the cost of operating the head office is allocated equally among the four divisions.

The income statement of the ABCD Conglomerate Corporation for the year ending December 31, 1983 appears as follows:

ABCD Conglomerate Corporation Income Statement December 31, 1983 (000 omitted)

Division	*A*	*B*	*C*	*D*	*Total*
Sales	$12,000	$8,000	$10,000	$5,000	$35,000
Cost of goods sold	8,000	6,000	5,000	3,000	22,000
Gross profit	$ 4,000	$2,000	$ 5,000	$2,000	$13,000
Divisional fixed costs	$ 2,000	$2,500	$ 4,000	$1,500	$10,000
Profit before corporate overhead	$ 2,000	$ (500)	$ 1,000	$ 500	$ 3,000
Corporate overhead	1,000	1,000	1,000	1,000	4,000
Net profit	$ 1,000	(1,500)	$ –0–	(500)	(1,000)

At first glance one would be inclined as the president of ABCD Conglomerate to order the dismemberment of divisions B, D, and even C. The justification for such an order would lie in the fact that none of these divisions appears to be making a contribution to the corporate bottom line. But a closer look at the picture reveals a truer, more complex situation.

Take the case of division D. It appears as though it is losing $500,000, and that its demise would only be fitting. Assume for the moment that division D is, in fact, terminated. One would expect that all the costs incurred by division D would no longer be borne by the firm. That is almost true. In fact, the corporate overhead allocated to division D would *not* cease to exist but would have to be paid by income produced from other divisions, since corporate overhead is independent of any division. The question therefore is not whether division D's bottom line shows a profit but rather whether division D is making a contribution toward the reduction of corporate overhead. Since division D reduces corporate overhead by $500,000 the division's life is justified. This can hardly be said of division B, which even before allocation of corporate overhead is generating a loss to the tune of $500,000. Division C's existence is fully warranted by the fact that it contributes generously to the reduction of corporate overhead.

SELF-TEST PROBLEMS

1. A factory manufactures electric clocks, which it sells for $35 per unit. The cost of raw materials and labor, and so on (variable cost) is $15 per unit. The fixed cost is $15 per unit. The fixed cost is $125,000. What is the break-even point?

2. A company has sales of $10 million on a volume of one million units. The fixed costs are $5 million and the profit for the period is $2 million. What is the variable cost per unit?

3. The Charles division of Sadie & Co., Inc. is headed by Renee Sawyer. Renee gets a bonus of $500 for every $100,000 of profit that her division generates. If the fixed costs are $500,000, the variable costs are $15 per unit, and the sales price is $18 per unit, how many units does the Charles division have to sell for Renee Sawyer to earn a bonus of $3000?

4. The EMKAY Calculator Corporation sells calculators for $10.50 to its wholesale distributors. In the most recent year EMKAY sold one million calculators, each with a variable cost of $7. If EMKAY had a profit of $3 million what is their fixed cost?

5. The Balkan Vending Company manufactures coin changers, which it sells for $1000 each. The variable cost of each machine is $880 and the fixed cost for operating the factory is $5040 per day. Sales in the most recent month have been sluggish, and Balkan management is considering the implementation of a sales promotion. The plan calls for stocking each new machine with $100 in nickels.

(a) If Balkan does not institute the promotion what is its break-even point?

(b) If the promotion is adopted what is now the break-even point?

CASE STUDY: THE KOWANGA INTERSTATE ELECTRIC COMPANY

The Kowanga Interstate Electric Company supplies electrical power to the entire Kowanga Valley region. Thanks to recent growth in the valley demand for electric power has risen so fast that Kowanga has not had sufficient time to construct a new generating plant to meet burgeoning demand. However, Kowanga has the opportunity to purchase electric power at $0.50 per kilowatt hour from a neighboring utility. To transport the power from the neighboring utility to Kowanga's territory, it will have to lay cables at a cost of $358,000. If Kowanga's price to its customers is $0.63 per kilowatt hour and the need for electricity from the neighboring utility is half a million kilowatt hours, should Kowanga lay the new cables?

Alternative Solutions It does not pay Kowanga to lay the new cables because the profit that would be generated is less than the cost of the new cables. Since each kilowatt hour costs $0.50 and is sold for $0.63 the contribution margin is:

```
 0.63
-0.50
-----
 0.13   contribution margin
```

Since we know that demand is 2.5 million kilowatts the total contribution margin is:

```
   0.13
x 2,500,000
-----------
  325,000     total contribution margin
```

Therefore, $325,000 is the total amount available to pay the fixed cost of laying the cable. Since the total contribution margin is less than the fixed cost, it is evident that the venture would not be profitable, as proposed.

It is important to note that our arrival at a numeric solution to a financial problem does not indicate the "end of the road." But it is a signpost along the path to a mutually advantageous solution. Kowanga's awareness that the proposed cables are not profitable does not necessarily mean that the deal should be dropped. Rather, Kowanga should consider other alternatives for getting the job done. For instance, it could appeal to its sister utility for assistance in financing the laying of the cables. Alternatively, the company could appeal to its consumers by informing them that it is impossible to furnish them electricity at current rates.

No matter which course of action Kowanga chooses, the calculation of break-even information is not the last step in the consideration. However, it is an important component of Kowanga's ability to judge a financial opportunity.

5 Foreign Currency Translations

Over the past twenty years the economic interdependence of nations has resulted in the proliferation of multinational corporations. Within the new environment it is necessary for almost every businessperson to be familiar with the differing customs and financial practices of the various nationalities. Among the issues of concern is the conversion of local currency into that of the firm's home country and vice versa. Since 1971 the Free World has been operating under a regime of floating exchange rates. Every day in the various money centers of the world (New York, London, Paris, Tokyo, and Zurich) currencies are bought and sold on exchanges that operate in much the same way as those that deal in stocks and bonds. The corporate executive whose firm operates in more than one country has a great stake in the activities of such exchanges. Fluctuations in the value of currencies affect every aspect of the firm's foreign performance. It is essential to be able to convert the value of one currency immediately into another currency's terms. For example, an American firm operating in Britain whose British subsidiary earned £100,000 on one day might have the equivalent of $219,900. Had the same earnings been announced just one day later their value might have been $221,250. Such day-to-day fluctuations are quite common. Obviously there is a need to convert from one currency to another quickly and accurately. Your calculator is ideally suited to this task. All that you need is the current rate of exchange between currencies.

CURRENCY CONVERSION

Below are the rates of exchange, expressed in dollars, for Friday, November 6, 1981.

Argentina (Peso)	.000162
Australia (Dollar)	1.1450
Austria (Schilling)	.0644
Belgium (Franc)	.0268
Bolivia (Peso)	.0404
Brazil (Cruzeiro)	.0087
Britain (Pound)	1.8760
Chile (Peso)	.0256
Colombia (Peso)	.0175
Denmark (Krone)	.1395
Egypt (Pound)	1.45
Ecuador (Sucre)	.0352
Finland (Mark)	.2293
France (Franc)	.1783
Greece (Drachma)	.0178
Holland (Guilder)	.4090
Hong Kong (Dollar)	.1764
India (Rupee)	.1093
Indonesia (Rupiah)	.00159
Iran (Rial)	.0124
Ireland (Pound)	1.5900
Israel (Shekel)	.0734
Italy (Lire)	.000842
Japan (Yen)	.004370
Jordan (Dinar)	3.0211
Kuwait (Dinar)	3.5536
Lebanon (Pound)	.2181
Mexico (Peso)	.0392
New Zealand (Dollar)	.8268
Norway (Krone)	.1706
Peru (Sol)	.002139
Philippines (Peso)	.1239
Portugal (Escudo)	.0156

Saudi Arabia (Riyal)	.2924
Singapore (Dollar)	.4794
South Africa (Rand)	1.0440
Spain (Peseta)	.0105
Sweden (Krona)	.1816
Switzerland (Franc)	.5593
Turkey (Lira)	.007851
Uruguay (Peso)	.0884
Venezuela (Bolivar)	.2331
West Germany (Mark)	.4505

Virtually all the freely floated currencies of the world are listed in alphabetical order by country, with the currency's name listed alongside. Some countries, such as the Soviet Union, will not honor a value for their currency established by the free market. Instead they peg the exchange rate of their currency at a particular level and conduct business only at that level.

To convert United States dollars into a foreign currency one merely *divides* the amount of dollars by the exchange rate. To convert a foreign currency into United States dollars one must *multiply* the foreign currency by the exchange rate. The above table may also be used to convert from one foreign currency into another foreign currency by first converting into United States dollars and then reconverting to the desired currency.

Suppose, for example, an American is taking a trip to Great Britain and wishes to convert $1000 into pounds sterling. The conversion may be calculated with the use of the above table and any calculator at all. As before we shall use both the HP-38 and the TI-MBA. Note that from the table shown, the rate of exchange is 1.8760 dollars to the pound.

HP-38

Step	*Key in*	*Display shows*
1	1000	1,000.
2	↑	1,000.00
3	1.876	1.876
4	÷	533.05

Answer: £533.05

TI-MBA

Step	*Key in*	*Display shows*
1	1000	1000.
2	÷	1000.
3	1.876	1.876
4	=	533.0490405

Answer: £533.05

As another example, if a resident of France went to visit Holland and took with him 5000 French francs, how many Dutch guilders would he receive for his money? Since we do not have a table to convert from French francs to Dutch guilders directly, we first convert the francs into American dollars and then convert from American dollars into Dutch guilders.

HP-38

Step	*Key in*	*Display shows*
1	5,000	5,000.
2	↑	5,000.00
3	.1783	0.1783
4	X	891.50
5	.4090	0.4090
6	÷	2,179.71

Answer: 2179.71 Dutch guilders

TI-MBA

Step	*Key in*	*Display shows*
1	5000	5000.
2	X	5000.
3	.1783	0.1783
4	÷	891.5
5	.4090	0.4090
6	=	2179.7066

Answer: 2179.71 Dutch guilders

HEDGING

If a company were expecting to receive quarterly income of $500,000 in foreign currency from a foreign subsidiary, the exact value of that currency would be in doubt. This is because within a period of three months (even within a period of three hours—or three minutes!) rates of exchange between currencies can fluctuate wildly, and at any given moment there is uncertainty about the currency's future value.

Fortunately, the financial markets provide methods of ensuring that a given rate of exchange holds steady for a specified period of time. One such method stems from the recent advent of the *financial futures market.* A futures contract is an agreement to deliver a specified amount of goods (in this case foreign currency) at a later date (perhaps three months) at an agreed upon price. If the company in question were to enter into such a contract it could receive the foreign currency at the contracted rate when the money arrives.

Another method to protect the value of a future currency conversion is to utilize the *financial options market.* In this market there are two types of contract: (a) a call and (b) a put.

A *call* is a contract in which the buyer pays the seller an amount of money. The buyer then has the right to buy a specific commodity at an agreed upon price within a specified time period.

A *put*, on the other hand, is a contract that allows the buyer to sell a particular commodity within a certain period at a contracted price. A put can be used to ensure that foreign currency coming in at a later date will be converted at a guaranteed rate. The cost of the put must be deducted from the firm's profit before a return on investment is calculated.

6 Analysis of Performance: Ratio Analysis

It is often necessary to analyze the past history of, and prospects for, a company's performance. Although gut feeling often plays a major role in such evaluations, a more objective viewpoint is obtained by an analysis of the data in a company's financial statements. Mostly, analysis consists of the construction of certain key ratios, which when taken together tell a corporation's "story." Unfortunately, there is no single ratio that can fully describe the current position of a company. Rather one must study the combination of many different ratios to get a clear picture. Particular ratios have greater significance for some industries than for others.

In this chapter we shall describe what are generally considered to be the most important financial and ratio terms. Though they are rather simple to calculate mathematically, if all these ratios were calculated for a single set of financial statements, a more complete analysis of the financial statements would still have to be made.

MARKET VALUE

It is impossible to predict what the price of a share of publicly traded stock will be at any future date; the price of a share of stock always fluctuates. Each movement in the price reflects a new evaluation by the market of a company's true value. If a company's stock sells for $10 per share and there are one million shares outstanding, the market value of the company is $10 million. Since the price of a share of stock is constantly changing, the market value of a company is correspondingly in flux. The excess of the market value over the value of the company as recorded on its balance sheet (the book value, which we shall discuss later) is referred to as goodwill. Goodwill represents the feeling of the market that the future prospects of the company are sufficiently high to warrant a premium over the book value.

Market value = Price per share X number of shares outstanding

Example 1 XYZ Company has 2,885,792 shares outstanding at a current price of $6 per share. What is the market value of XYZ Company's stock?

HP-38

Step	*Key in*	*Display shows*
1	2885792	2,885,792.
2	↑	2,885,792.00
3	6	6.
4	X	17,314,752.00

Answer: $17,314,752

TI-MBA

Step	*Key in*	*Display shows*
1	2885792	2885792.
2	X	2885792.
3	6	6.
4	=	17314752.

Answer: $17,314,752

Example 2 Galley Razor Corporation has 3,892,435 shares of its stock outstanding. Galley's shares, which trade on the New York Stock Exchange, were last sold for 18 5/8 ($18.625). Determine the current market value of Galley's shares.

HP-38

Step	*Key in*	*Display shows*
1	3892435	3,892,435.
2	↑	3,892,435.00

Step	*Key in*	*Display shows*
3	18.625	18.625
4	X	72,496,601.88

Answer: $72,496,601.88

TI-MBA

Step	*Key in*	*Display shows*
1	3892435	3892435.
2	X	3892435.
3	18.625	18.625
4	=	72496601.88

Answer: $72,496,601.88

EARNINGS PER SHARE

Every shareholder of a company is entitled to a share in the profits. Sometimes the profits are distributed to the company's shareholders in the form of dividends; other times the profits are retained by the company for further investment in its future. Frequently, some profits are distributed as dividends to the shareholders, while the remainder of the profits are retained within the company's coffers. Regardless of whether the profit id distributed or not, each and every share of common stock can be said to "own" a share of the profits. The amount of profit allocated to each share of common stock is the *earnings per share* (EPS). EPS is calculated by dividing the average number of shares outstanding throughout the year into the profits for the year. This is known as *primary* EPS.

$$\text{Earnings per share} = \frac{\text{Profit}}{\text{Number of shares outstanding}}$$

Many companies also issue securities known as warrants and convertible debentures. A warrant is a security that entitles the holder to buy a share of stock from the company at a specified price. Sometimes warrants have an expiration date; otherwise they are valid in perpetuity. A convertible debenture is very much like a bond in that it is an interest-bearing security (usually at a fixed rate) with a predetermined life. What distinguishes a convertible debenture from a bond is that a convertible debenture can be exchanged for a fixed number of shares of stock in the company.

If a company has warrants and/or convertible debentures outstanding the possibility exists that additional shares of stock will have to be issued at some point in the future. Since the conversion of both warrants and convertible debentures into shares of stock can reduce the EPS. In many financial statements this potential "dilution" is reflected through the presentation of an additional EPS figure, known as *fully diluted* earnings per share. Fully diluted EPS is a calculation of the EPS assuming all the warrants and convertible debentures that would have a substantive effect on the number of shares outstanding are exchanged for shares of common stock.

Example 1 Earl P. Snowdon, Inc. earned $3,526,000 in its most recent fiscal year. If the company has 5,756,000 shares of its stock outstanding, what is its earnings per share?

HP-38

Step	*Key in*	*Display shows*
1	3526000	3,526,000.
2	↑	3,526,000.00
3	5756000	5,756,000.
4	÷	0.61

Answer: $0.61 per share

TI-MBA

Step	*Key in*	*Display shows*
1	3526000	3526000.
2	÷	3526000.
3	5756000	5756000.
4	=	.612578179

Answer: $0.61 per share

Example 2 Sternly Stan Corporation has 3,658,924 shares outstanding, and according to its latest quarterly report it earned $555,000 in the last three months. What was its quarterly earnings per share?

HP-38

Step	*Key in*	*Display shows*
1	555000	555,000.
2	↑	555,000.

Step	*Key in*	*Display shows*
3	3658942	3,658,942
4	÷	0.15

Answer: $0.15 per share

TI-MBA

Step	*Key in*	*Display shows*
1	555000	555000.
2	÷	555000.
3	3658942	3658942.
4	=	0.151683192

Answer: $0.15 per share

PRICE TO EARNINGS RATIO

The price of a share of stock often bears a strong relationship to the primary EPS of a company. Odds are that if earnings rise, or if earnings are expected to rise, the share's price will move upward. Even so, as earnings change, the relationship between EPS and market price remains the same. This relationship is generally referred to as the *price-to-earnings ratio*, or P-E ratio. The P-E ratio is calculated by dividing the primary EPS into the market price. Many financial analysts want to know the range of the P-E ratio over the course of time, generally for a one-year period. To calculate this range you take both the highest and the lowest price a share of the company's stock reached over the period and divide each of them separately by the EPS to arrive at the high and low for the P-E ratio.

All publicly held companies with more than a minimum number of shareholders announce their earnings both annually and quarterly. The P-E ratio is a crucial figure, not only at the end of the year, when annual earnings are announced, but throughout the year, when only quarterly earnings are available. Many investors would like to know the P-E ratio based on the preceding 12 months' earnings, regardless of whether the most recent earnings announcement was one of annual or quarterly earnings. To produce a P-E ratio using a full year's earnings after only the first quarter's earnings have been announced, you take the prior year's earnings, subtract from it the earnings for the first quarter of *that* year, and add the *current* year's first quarter's earnings. This figure is known as *trailing twelve months' earnings* (TTM earnings). The formula

$$\frac{\text{Market price}}{\text{TTM earnings}}$$

gives a P–E ratio based on the most recently completed 12-month period.

Example 1 Kraus Elementals Corporation's shares are currently selling at $8.50 per share. In the most recent fiscal year Kraus earned $2,538,000 or $1.12 per share. Calculate Kraus's P–E ratio.

HP-38

Step	*Key in*	*Display shows*
1	8.5	8.50
2	↑	8.50
3	1.12	1.12
4	÷	7.59

Answer: 7.6

TI-MBA

Step	*Key in*	*Display shows*
1	8.5	8.5
2	÷	8.5
3	1.12	1.12
4	=	7.589285714

Answer: 7.6

Example 2 On March 31 Degel Inc. announced that in the three months ended on that day it earned $0.62 per share. Degel management made the announcement with great delight since in the three months ending March 31 of the previous year its earnings were only $0.03 per share. If Degel earned $1.50 per share in the year ending December 31 and the share price is currently 9–1/8, what is the P–E ratio based on trailing twelve months' earnings?

HP-38

Step	*Key in*	*Display shows*
1	9.125	9.125
2	↑	9.13
3	1.5	1.5
4	↑	1.50
5	.62	0.62
6	+	2.12
7	.03	0.03
8	−	2.09
9	÷	4.37

Answer: 4.4

TI-MBA

Step	*Key in*	*Display shows*
1	1.5	1.5
2	+	1.5
3	.62	0.62
4	−	2.12
5	.03	0.03
6	=	2.09
7	STO 1	2.09
8	9.125	9.125
9	÷	9.125
10	RCL 1	2.09
11	=	4.366028708

Answer: 4.4

NET PROFIT MARGIN

A company hopes that out of each sale it makes a certain amount of profit is generated. If a company makes a sale of $3, of which $0.15 is profit, it can be said that for each dollar of the sale five cents of profit was made. The company's net profit margin for this sale is therefore 5 percent. To obtain the company's overall net profit margin one need only divide the net profit by net sales. The percentage obtained in this calculation is the average number of cents of profit in each dollar of sales for the company as a whole.

$$\text{Net profit margin} = \frac{\text{Net profit}}{\text{Sales}}$$

Example 1 Keeva Products earned $572,000 in profit for a given year. Its sales during the same year were $10.5 million. Find the net profit margin.

HP-38

Step	*Key in*	*Display shows*
1	572000	572,000.
2	↑	572,000.00
3	10500000	10,500,000.
4	f3	10,500,000.00
5	÷	0.054

Answer: 5.4 percent

Notice that step 4 rounds the percentage to three places.

TI-MBA

Step	*Key in*	*Display shows*
1	572000	572000.
2	÷	572000.
3	10500000	10500000.
4	=	0.05447619

Answer: 5.4 percent

Example 2 The Union Jack Flag Company registered sales of $598,650 and a profit of $15,500. Find the net profit margin.

HP-38

Step	*Key in*	*Display shows*
1	f3	0.000
2	15500	15,500.
3	↑	15,500.000
4	598650	598,650.
5	÷	0.026

Answer: 2.6 percent

TI-MBA

Step	*Key in*	*Display shows*
1	15500	15500.
2	÷	15500.
3	598650	598650.
4	=	.0258915894

Answer: 2.6 percent

GROSS PROFIT MARGIN

Gross profit is a term we have already discussed under a different name, contribution margin. Simply stated, gross profit is sales less variable costs. Gross profit margin is the amount of each dollar of sales that is gross profit. Gross profit margin is calculated by dividing gross profit by sales.

$$\text{Gross profit margin} = \frac{\text{Gross profit}}{\text{Sales}}$$

Example 1 Gray's Caterers posted sales of $10,540,000 with a cost of sales of $6,324,000. Find the gross profit margin.

HP-38

Step	*Key in*	*Display shows*
1	10540000	10,540,000.
2	STO 1	10,540,000.00
3	6324000	6,324,000.
4	−	4,216,000.00
5	RCL 1	10,540,000.00
6	÷	0.40

Answer: 40 percent

TI-MBA

Step	*Key in*	*Display Shows*
1	10540000	10540000.
2	STO 1	10540000.
3	−	10540000.
4	6324000	6324000.
5	=	4216000.
6	÷	4216000
7	RCL 1	10540000.
8	=	0.4

Answer: 40 percent

Example 2 Emmett Brothers has a gross profit of $4,580,000, and sales of $8,423,000. Find the gross profit margin.

HP-38

Step	*Key in*	*Display shows*
1	4580000	4,580,000.
2	↑	4,580,000.

Step	*Key in*	*Display shows*
3	8423000	8423000.
4	÷	0.54

Answer: 54 percent

TI-MBA

Step	*Key in*	*Display shows*
1	4580000	4580000.
2	÷	4580000.
3	8423000	8423000.
4	=	0.543749258

Answer: 54 percent

RETURN ON EQUITY

The balance sheet, the financial picture of a corporation, is divided into three sections:

1. Assets, or economic resources
2. Liabilities, or debt
3. Equity, or the resources invested in the company by the owners.

As in any investment the investor needs to know the return on the investment. Normally this is calculated by dividing the earnings of the investment by the amount invested. The return on a company is equal to the net income divided by the shareholders' equity, as represented by the third section of the balance sheet, referred to as return on equity (ROE).

$$\text{Return on equity} = \frac{\text{Net income}}{\text{Shareholders' equity}}$$

Example 1 Susan Sweaters Company has a total shareholders' equity of $18,000,000. If its net income is $542,000 what is the return on equity?

HP-38

Step	*Key in*	*Display shows*
1	542000	542,000.
2	↑	542,000.00

Step	*Key in*	*Display shows*
3	18000000	18,000,000.
4	÷	0.03

Answer: 3 percent

TI-MBA

Step	*Key in*	*Display shows*
1	542000	542000.
2	÷	542000.
3	18000000	18000000.
4	=	.0301111111

Answer: 3 percent

Example 2 Esplanade Enterprises announced earnings of $14,000,000 with equity of $207,982,000. Find the return on equity.

HP-38

Step	*Key in*	*Display shows*
1	14000000	14,000,000.
2	↑	14,000,000.00
3	207982000.	207,982,000.
4	÷	0.07

Answer: 7 percent

TI-MBA

Step	*Key in*	*Display shows*
1	14000000	14000000.
2	÷	14000000.
3	207982000	207982000.
4	=	.0673135175

Answer: 7 percent

RETURN ON AVERAGE EQUITY

Over the course of a year the earnings retained by a corporation (those not paid out in dividends) are added to the existing equity. Hence, for a profitable corporation, the value of the equity increases over the year. Since the earnings were generated as the equity was growing it is often not considered appropriate to calculate return on equity using the equity at the end of the year. Rather the return is calculated on the *average* equity. Average equity is calculated by adding the equity at the end of the year to the equity at the beginning of the year and dividing the result by 2. The return on average equity is simply net income divided by average equity.

$$\text{Return on average equity} = \frac{\text{Net income}}{(\text{Equity at beginning of year} + \text{equity at end of year}) \div 2}$$

Example Mitsuyan Corporation, a highly regarded orange growing cooperative, announces earnings of $290,000 and a record shareholders' equity of $3,626,733. The previous year Mitsuyan reported earnings of $240,000 and shareholders' equity of $3,373,000. Find the return on average equity.

HP-38

Step	*Key in*	*Display shows*
1	290000	290,000.
2	↑	290,000.00
3	3626733	3,626,733
4	↑	3,626,733.00
5	3373000	3,373,000.
6	+	6,999,733.00
7	2	2.
8	÷	3,499,866.50
9	÷	0.08

Answer: 8 percent

TI-MBA

Step	*Key in*	*Display shows*
1	3626733	3626733.
2	+	3626733.
3	3373000	3373000.
4	=	6999733.
5	÷	6999733.
6	2	2.
7	=	3499866.5
8	STO 1	3499866.5
9	290000	290000.
10	÷	290000.
11	RCL 1	3499866.5
12	=	.0828603034

Answer: 8 percent

RETURN ON COMMON EQUITY

Though companies have different types of stock, the usual distinction is between *common stock* and *preferred stock*;

within each of these types there may be different categories of stock. Normally, a share of preferred stock is similar to a bond in that it has a fixed rate of return and does not entitle the holder to voting rights in the corporation. Therefore it is usually held that preferred stockholders are *not* owners of the corporation.

The return on equity calculations performed above determined the return on all the equity, including that of the preferred stockholders. But it is often desirable to figure the return on equity for just the common shareholders. This entails removing from net income any dividends accrued to the preferred shareholders and dividing the remainder by the equity owned by the shareholders of common stock. For example, if a company earned $539,000 and owes $26,000 to its preferred shareholders and the value of the shareholders' equity after removing the balance sheet value of the preferred stock is $10,000,000 the return on common equity is:

$$\frac{539{,}000 - 26{,}000}{10{,}000{,}000} = 5.1 \text{ percent}$$

Example Melakh Salt Company has two types of stock outstanding. The first, its preferred stock, pays a dividend of $2.35 per share for each of the 650,000 shares outstanding, for a total of $1,527,500 in preferred dividends per year. The second, its common stock, has 30,000,000 shares outstanding, and in the most recent fiscal year Melakh earned $6,350,000. The common shareholders' equity on Melakh's balance sheet is $112,500,000. Calculate the return on common equity.

HP-38

Step	*Key in*	*Display shows*
1	6350000	6,350,000.
2	↑	6,350,000.00
3	1527500	1,527,500.
4	–	4,822,500.00
5	112500000	112,500,000.
6	÷	0.04

Answer: 4 percent

TI-MBA

Step	*Key in*	*Display shows*
1	6350000	6350000.
2	−	6350000
3	1527500	1527500.
4	=	4822500.
5	÷	4822500.
6	112500000	112500000.
7	=	.0428666667

Answer: 4 percent

RETURN ON AVERAGE COMMON EQUITY

As described above, the earnings of a company usually increase the equity on the balance sheet. That is why return on average equity is often preferable to return on equity as an evaluative measure. Similarly, return on average common equity is often preferable to return on common equity as a measure of a company's performance. *Average common equity* is computed by adding the common equity at the beginning of the year to the common equity at the end of the year, and then dividing the results by two. The return is that number divided into net profit less preferred dividends, the same as for return on common equity.

$$\text{Return on average common equity} = \frac{\text{Net profit} - \text{preferred dividends}}{(\text{Equity at beginning year} + \text{equity at end of year}) \div 2}$$

Example Gary Nimm Corporation, a renowned nut processor, pays preferred dividends totaling $80,000 per year. The previous year Gary Nimm earned a profit of $235,000 and had a shareholders' equity of $2 million, compared to the previous year's shareholders' equity of $1,815,000. Compute the return on average common equity.

HP-38

Step	*Key in*	*Display shows*
1	235000	235,000.
2	↑	235,000.
3	80000	80,000.

Step	*Key in*	*Display shows*
4	–	155,000.00
5	2000000	2,000,000.
6	↑	2,000,000.00
7	1815000	1,815,000.
8	+	3,815,000.00
9	2	2.
10	÷	1,907,500.00
11	÷	0.08

Answer: 8 percent

TI-MBA

Step	*Key in*	*Display shows*
1	2000000	2000000.
2	+	2000000.
3	1815000	1815000.
4	=	3815000.
5	÷	3815000.
6	2	2.
7	=	1907500.
8	STO 1	1907500.
9	235000	235000.
10	–	235000.
11	80000	80000.
12	=	155000.
13	÷	155000.
14	RCL 1	1907500.
15	=	.0812581913

Answer: 8 percent

RETURN ON TOTAL ASSETS

A firm's assets are the tools it employs to build a successful future for itself in the competitive environment. A firm's assets are owned by the company's creditors and the company's shareholders. At all times both those parties are concerned with how well the firm is managing its assets to produce income, or return.

Return on total assets is calculated by dividing net income by total assets. This ratio, expressed as a percentage, indicates how well the company is employing its assets. The higher the percentage, the greater the return.

$$\text{Return on total assets} = \frac{\text{Net income}}{\text{Total assets}}$$

Example 1 Kavod Corporation reported total assets of $150,000 and earnings of $22,537. What is their return on total assets?

HP-38

Step	*Key in*	*Display shows*
1	22537	22,537.
2	↑	22,537.00
3	150000	150,000.
4	÷	0.15

Answer: 15 percent

TI-MBA

Step	*Key in*	*Display shows*
1	22537	22537.
2	÷	22537.
3	150000	150000.
4	=	.1502466667

Answer: 15 percent

Example 2 Lawrence Lakeside Industries posted earnings of $18,478,500 against total assets of $146,592,450. Find the return on total assets.

HP-38

Step	*Key in*	*Display shows*
1	18478500	18,478,500.
2	↑	18,478,500.00
3	146592450	146,592,450.
4	÷	0.13

Answer: 13 percent

TI-MBA

Step	*Key in*	*Display shows*
1	18478500	18478500.
2	÷	18478500.
3	146592450	146592450.
4	=	.1260535587

Answer: 13 percent

RETURN ON AVERAGE ASSETS

Over time the value of a firm's assets changes in the normal course of business. The return on total assets indicates how well a company utilized the assets it owned at a specific point in time. The return, however, is not generated at a specific point in time but rather over a period of time. It is therefore appropriate to consider the average value of the assets during the time the return was earned.

Average assets is the total assets at the beginning of the period plus the total assets at the end of the period divided by 2. When that number is divided into net income the resulting number is the return on average assets.

$$\text{Return on average assets} = \frac{\text{Net income}}{(\text{Assets at the beginning of the period} + \text{assets at the end of the period}) \div 2}$$

Example 1 American Spirits Corporation has assets at the beginning of the year of \$16,572,000 and total assets at the end of the year of \$18,492,500. During the year the company earned \$856,485. Find the return on average assets.

HP-38

Step	*Key in*	*Display shows*
1	16572000	16,572,000.
2	↑	16,572,000.
3	18492500	18,492,500.
4	+	35,064,500.00
5	2	2.
6	÷	17,532,250.00
7	856485	856,485.
8	x ⪆ y	17,532,250.00
9	÷	0.05

Answer: 5 percent

TI-MBA

Step	*Key in*	*Display shows*
1	16572000	16572000.
2	+	16572000.

Step	*Key in*	*Display shows*
3	18492500	18492500.
4	=	35064500.
5	÷	35064500.
6	2	2.
7	=	17532250.
8	STO 1	17532250.
9	856485	856485.
10	÷	856485.
11	RCL 1	17532250.
12	=	.0488519728

Answer: 5 percent

Example 2 Mayer Messenger Corporation has income for the year of $55,874,263. At the beginning of the year the firm had $289,075,400 in total assets, and they ended the year with $294,486,750 in total assets. Find the return on average assets.

HP-38

Step	*Key in*	*Display shows*
1	55874263	55,874,263.
2	↑	55,874,263.00
3	289075400	289,075,400.
4	↑	289,075,400.0
5	294486750	294,486,750.
6	+	583,562,150.0
7	2	2.
8	÷	291,781,075.0
9	÷	0.19

Answer: 19 percent

TI-MBA

Step	*Key in*	*Display shows*
1	289075400	289075400.
2	+	289075400.
3	294486750	294486750.
4	=	583562150.
5	÷	583562150.
6	2	2.
7	=	291781075.
8	STO 1	291781075.
9	55874263	55874263.
10	÷	55874263.
11	RCL 1	291781075.
12	=	.1914937869

Answer: 19 percent

BOOK VALUE PER SHARE

You may be aware that assets minus liabilities equals shareholders' equity. Every shareholder owns a portion of the equity corresponding to the number of shares owned. Although the market value of a share of stock often reflects the balance sheet value of the equity, the two numbers are not necessarily the same. When equity is divided by the number of shares outstanding, the book value per share of the company is obtained. This figure is often used for comparison with the market price.

$$\text{Book value per share} = \frac{\text{Assets} - \text{liabilities}}{\text{Shares outstanding}}$$

Example 1 Equity Corporation has total assets of $5,420,000 and total liabilities of $4,120,500. If there are 12,650,000 shares outstanding, what is the book value per share?

HP-38

Step	*Key in*	*Display shows*
1	5420000	5,420,000.
2	↑	5,420,000.00
3	4120500	4,120,500.
4	−	1,299,500.00
5	12650000	12,650,000.
6	÷	0.10

Answer: $0.10

TI-MBA

Step	*Key in*	*Display shows*
1	5420000	5420000.
2	−	5420000
3	4120500	4120500.
4	=	1299500.
5	÷	1299500
6	12650000	12650000.
7	=	.1027272727

Answer: $0.10

Example 2 Parker Paint Products has total shareholders' equity of $85,350,000. With 47,289,652 shares outstanding find the book value per share.

HP-38

Step	*Key in*	*Display shows*
1	85350000	85,350,000.
2	↑	85,350,000.00
3	47289652	47,289,652.
4	=	1.80

Answer: $1.80

TI-MBA

Step	*Key in*	*Display shows*
1	85350000	85350000.
2	÷	85350000
3	47289652	47289652.
4	=	1.804834597

Answer: $1.80

DIVIDEND YIELD

Many investors want to know what return they are getting for the money they invested in a share of stock. Often, the return consists solely of cash dividends received. In that case, the annual yield is the dividends received during a 12-month period divided by the cost of the stock.

Sometimes, while searching for stocks in which to invest, the investor likes to know what the range of the dividend yield has been in the past. To calculate this all you have to do is take the sum of the dividends and divide it by both the highest and the lowest price the shares reached, which gives the range.

$$\text{Dividend yield} = \frac{\text{Dividends paid in year}}{\text{Price paid per share}}$$

Example 1 Gazellers Corporation pays a dividend of $0.80 per share. If the current price of the shares is 16 5/8, what is the dividend yield?

HP-38

Step	*Key in*	*Display shows*
1	.8	0.8
2	↑	0.80
3	16.625	16.625
4	÷	0.05

Answer: 5 percent

TI-MBA

Step	*Key in*	*Display shows*
1	.8	.8
2	÷	.8
3	16.625	16.625
4	=	.0481203008

Answer: 5 percent

Example 2 Moriah Machinery Corporation's stock is selling for $40.25 per share and pays a dividend of $6.00 per year. Compute the dividend yield.

HP-38

Step	*Key in*	*Display shows*
1	6	6.
2	↑	6.00
3	40.25	40.25
4	÷	0.15

Answer: 15 percent

TI-MBA

Step	*Key in*	*Display shows*
1	6	6.
2	÷	6.
3	40.25	40.25
4	=	0.149068323

Answer: 15 percent

DEBT TO TOTAL ASSETS RATIO

There are basically two ways a company may obtain funds for future growth and expansion. The first is *equity*, the amount of money invested by shareholders and the profit generated from the investment (other than the profit paid out in dividends). The second method is *debt*, any money owed by a company to its creditors, which may well include accounts payable to suppliers of raw materials to the company, debts to banks, debts to bondholders, and so on.

A company's objective in obtaining capital is the proper balance of debt and equity. It might seem as if the ideal proportion of debt to equity would be the same for every company. Unfortunately, this can never be so. The differing nature of industries and the various structures of companies dictate that a different balance of debt and equity be designed for almost every corporation.

Both debt and equity have their advantages and drawbacks as sources of capital. Take the case of an entrepreneur who wants to start a new venture for which he needs $2 million. Assume that he has decided to issue 1.5 million shares of stock and intends to keep 500,000 shares of stock for himself in recognition of his contribution of time and effort to the firm. One option is to sell the remaining one million shares at $2.00 apiece. If he follows that option and the company earns $1.5 million in profit during the first year, the earnings per share will be $1.50. If, on the other hand, he borrows the entire $2 million at 5 percent interest (after tax), and the company earns the same $1.5 million, he will pay $100,000 (5 percent of $2 million) to his creditors and have $1.4 million to be divided up only by the 500,000 shares he himself owns, giving him earnings per share of $2.80.

The advantage of "leveraging" a company through the use of debt is evidenced in the earnings per share figure in the above example. Another advantage of debt is that the interest paid to creditors is a tax-deductible expense as opposed to the dividends paid to shareholders, which are not tax deductible.

The above example seems to indicate that at all times a company should issue debt rather than sell stock (equity). This, however, is not always true. The rate of interest that a company must pay on its debt depends upon its creditors' perception of the likelihood of repayment. The less likely a repayment, the higher the interest cost to the company. The more interest expense a company has, the less likely it is that it will be able to meet that interest expense. Hence it is not always wise for a company to obtain all of its capital needs through the issuance of debt, since that will cause creditors to demand a high rate of return on the debt, which the company may not be able to support.

Equity, on the other hand, enables a company to obtain capital without having to provide an immediate return to the suppliers of the capital. You are probably aware of companies whose stock pays no dividend. Those companies' shareholders have given their capital to the company so that it may grow and prosper without being burdened by heavy interest expenses.

What equity investors hope for is either (a) to receive dividends at some future date that are larger than the interest payments would have been had they loaned the money to the company, or (b) a marked appreciation in the price of the stock based on the market's perception of the company's prospects for the future.

Some companies, whose future income can be easily determined, are more suited to debt financing since creditors are more certain of repayment. Other companies, whose future income is dependent upon many factors such as the course of the general economy, the weather, or the intensity of sunspots, are less suited to debt financing.

Amounts included under the category of debt vary from company to company and even from analyst to analyst. For example, some include amounts owed to suppliers of raw materials, short-term debt to banks, and so on, while others exclude such short-term borrowing. Neither approach is absolutely correct, and judgment must be used in deciding which course to take. We will categorize as debt everything in the liabilities section of a balance sheet.

In view of the fact that the balance of debt and equity is so crucial to a company, ratios that measure the balance are necessary. One such ratio is that of debt to total assets, which is simply:

$$\frac{\text{Debt}}{\text{Total assets}}$$

The result of this calculation gives the proportion of all the assets that are financed by debt.

Example 1 Cooper Nuts Corporation has total assets of \$3,490,000 and total liabilities of \$1,895,500. Compute the ratio of debt to total assets.

HP-38

Step	*Key in*	*Display shows*
1	1895500	1,895,500
2	↑	1,895,500.00
3	3490000	3,490,000.
4	÷	0.54

Answer: 54 percent

TI-MBA

Step	*Key in*	*Display shows*
1	1895500	1895500
2	÷	1895500.
3	3490000	3490000.
4	=	.5431232092

Answer: 54 percent

Example 2 G. S. Bagels claims total liabilities of $540,000 and total shareholders' equity of $364,000. Find the debt to equity ratio.

HP-38

Step	*Key in*	*Display shows*
1	2400000	2,400,000.
2	↑	2,400,000.00
3	3120000	3,120,000.
4	÷	0.77

Answer: 77 percent

TI-MBA

Step	*Key in*	*Display shows*
1	2400000	2400000.
2	÷	2400000
3	3120000	3120000
4	=	.7692307692

Answer: 77 percent

DEBT TO EQUITY RATIO

The debt to equity ratio compares the relative size of a company's debt financing to its equity financing. It is calculated by:

$$\frac{\text{Debt}}{\text{Equity}}$$

Example 1 The total debt of McWilliams Products is $2,980,000, while their total equity is $3,150,000. Compute their debt to equity ratio.

HP-38

Step	*Key in*	*Display shows*
1	2980000	2,980,000
2	↑	2,980,000.00
3	3150000	3,150,000.
4	÷	0.95

Answer: 0.95: 1

TI-MBA

Step	*Key in*	*Display shows*
1	2980000	2980000.
2	÷	2980000
3	3150000	3150000
4	=	0.946031746

Answer: 0.95: 1

Example 2 G. S. Bagels claims total liabilities of $540,000 and total shareholders' equity of $364,000. Find the debt to equity ratio.

HP-38

Step	*Key in*	*Display shows*
1	540000	540,000.
2	↑	540,000.00
3	364000	364,000.
4	÷	1.48

Answer: 1.48: 1

TI-MBA

Step	*Key in*	*Display shows*
1	540000	540000.
2	÷	540000
3	364000	364000.
4	=	1.483516484

Answer: 1.48: 1

LONG-TERM DEBT TO TOTAL CAPITALIZATION RATIO

The phrase *long-term debt* usually refers to the debt of a company with a maturity greater than one year (and usually includes deferred taxes). The total capitalization of a company is the long-term debt plus equity. Total capitalization refers to the money a company is certain to have over an extended period of time. The calculation of the long-term debt to total capitalization ratio is:

$$\frac{\text{Long-term debt}}{\text{Total capitalization}}$$

Its significance lies in its ability to describe the proportion of the company's permanent capital upon which interest must be paid.

Example Pearson's Pickles Inc. has total long-term debt (including capitalized leases) of $85,500,000 and total equity of $210,450,000. Find the ratio of long-term debt to total capitalization.

HP-38

Step	*Key in*	*Display shows*
1	85500000	85,500,000.
2	↑	85,500,000.00
3	↑	85,500,000.00
4	210450000	210,450,000
5	+	295,950,000.0
6	÷	0.29

Answer: 29 percent

TI-MBA

Step	*Key in*	*Display shows*
1	85500000	85500000.
2	STO 1	85500000.
3	+	85500000.
4	210450000	210450000.
5	=	295950000.
6	STO 2	295950000.
7	RCL 1	85500000.
8	÷	85500000
9	RCL 2	295950000.
10	=	.2889001521
11		

Answer: 29 percent

SALES PER SQUARE FOOT

In certain industries space is a constraining factor. A department store, for example, is limited in its capacity to sell goods by the physical space of the building it occupies. Therefore, a good measure of the store's performance is how much sales it generates given the amount of space available. The sales per square foot ratio describes how well a company performs in an average square foot of space. You can well imagine that a store with wide aisles and uncluttered racks does not do too well by this measure. On the other hand, the world-renowned store Bloomingdale's, to cite an example, is always crowded with merchandise and eager buyers and probably does very well indeed by this measure.

$$\text{Sales per square foot} = \frac{\text{Amount of sales}}{\text{Number of square feet}}$$

Example 1 Murdock Fashions Inc. owns a department store with an area of 4500 square feet. In the most recent year sales were $256,000. Calculate the sales per square foot.

HP-38

Step	*Key in*	*Display shows*
1	256000	256,000.
2	↑	256,000.00
3	4500	4,500.
4	÷	56.89

Answer: $56.89

TI-MBA

Step	*Key in*	*Display shows*
1	256000	256000.
2	÷	256000
3	4500	4500.
4	=	56.88888889

Answer: $56.89

Example 2 Jacqueline Retailers owns two stores, one on the east side and one on the west side of town. The east side store has sales of $1,187,000 and a total area of 4432 square feet. The store on the west side has sales of $2,468,000 and occupies an area of 8985 square feet. Which store has the greater sales per square foot?

HP-38

East Side Store

Step	*Key in*	*Display shows*
1	1187000	1,187,000
2	↑	1,187,000.00
3	4432	4,432
4	÷	267.82

West Side Store

Step	*Key in*	*Display shows*
5	2468000	2,468,000.
6	↑	2,468,000.00
7	8985	8,985.
8	÷	274.68

Answer: West Side store ($274.68) has more sales per square foot than East Side store ($267.82).

TI-MBA

East Side Store

Step	*Key in*	*Display shows*
1	1187000	1187000
2	÷	1187000.
3	4432	4432
4	=	267.82491

West Side Store

Step	*Key in*	*Display shows*
5	2468000	2468000
6	÷	2468000.
7	8985	8985
8	=	274.68002

Answer: West Side store ($274.68) has more sales per square foot than East Side store ($267.82).

CURRENT RATIO

Current assets are those that will, under normal practices, turn into cash within one year. They include but are not limited to bank accounts, marketable securities, accounts receivable, inventories, and cash itself. Current liabilities are those debts that will, under normal circumstances, be paid off within one year. They include but are not restricted to accounts payable, wages payable, dividends payable, taxes payable, and bank loans payable.

To avoid insolvency a company's current assets must be greater than its current liabilities. This is to ensure that the repayment of maturing debt can be met by the incoming cash flow. If you divide the current assets by the current liabilities the resulting figure is referred to as the current ratio, which reflects the ability of the company to meet its debts over the coming year.

$$\text{Current ratio} = \frac{\text{Current assets}}{\text{Current liabilities}}$$

Example 1 Kadesh Brothers's most recent balance sheet lists its current assets as $4,582,000 and current liabilities as $942,000. Find the current ratio.

HP-38

Step	*Key in*	*Display shows*
1	4582000	4,582,000.
2	↑	4,582,000
3	942000	942,000.
4	÷	4.86

Answer: 4.9

TI-MBA

Step	*Key in*	*Display shows*
1	4582000	4582000.
2	÷	4582000
3	942000	942000.
4	=	4.864118896

Answer: 4.9

Example 2 Mercer Manufacturers has a current ratio of 1.27 and current liabilities of $485,000. Find the current assets.

HP-38

Step	*Key in*	*Display shows*
1	485000	485,000
2	↑	485,000.00
3	1.27	1.27
4	X	615,950.00

Answer: $615,950

TI-MBA

Step	*Key in*	*Display shows*
1	485000	485000.
2	×	485000.
3	1.27	1.27
4	=	615950.

Answer: $615,950

QUICK (ACID TEST) RATIO

Certain kinds of current assets revert to cash more quickly than others. These are known as highly "liquid" assets. They are cash itself, marketable securities, and accounts receivable. The quick ratio, which is calculated as:

$$\frac{\text{Cash} + \text{Marketable securities} + \text{Accounts receivable}}{\text{Current liabilities}}$$

describes how well a business can pay off its current liabilities from the cash it could generate out of its most liquid assets.

Example 1 Wearever Industries has cash and marketable securities of $3,250,000 and accounts receivable of $5,785,000. If Wearever's current liabilities are $8,214,000, what is their quick ratio?

HP-38

Step	*Key in*	*Display shows*
1	3250000	3,250,000.
2	↑	3,250,000.00
3	5785000	5,785,000.
4	+	9,035,000.00
5	8214000	8,214,000.
6	÷	1.10

Answer: 1.1

TI-MBA

Step	*Key in*	*Display shows*
1	3250000	3250000.
2	+	3250000.
3	5785000	5785000.

Step	*Key in*	*Display shows*
4	=	9035000.
5	÷	9035000.
6	8214000	8214000.
7	=	1.099951303

Answer: 1.1

Example 2 Kippa Headwear Inc. has a quick ratio of 1.86. If the total amount of their cash, marketable securities, and accounts receivable is $4,187,500, what are their current liabilities?

HP-38

Step	*Key in*	*Display shows*
1	4187500	4,187,500.
2	↑	4,187,500.
3	1.86	1.86
4	÷	2,251,344.09

Answer: $2,251,344

TI-MBA

Step	*Key in*	*Display shows*
1	4187500	4187500.
2	÷	4187500
3	1.86	1.86
4	=	2251344.086

Answer: $2,251,344

INVENTORY TURNOVER

Inventory management is often a crucial element in the success or failure of a company. Ideally, a company should have an adequate inventory on hand of the goods that are in demand and a minimum of those that turn out to be unpopular. Even among the fast-moving items it is important not to stock to excess. An inventory that is too large requires additional financing, which entails further interest expense and is therefore counterproductive.

Financial analysts have devised a method to portray the speed with which a company is able to move its inventory. The result of that calculation is a measure of how many times the value of the inventory is sold over the course of a year.

Since inventory is recorded on the balance sheet in terms of its cost, and not in terms of its selling price, it is sometimes considered more appropriate to arrive at inventory turnover using cost of goods sold rather than sales because it seems more reasonable to associate inventory with cost price rather than selling price.

$$\text{Inventory turnover} = \frac{\text{Sales (or cost of goods sold)}}{\text{Inventory}}$$

Example 1 Pick Pickle Co. racked up sales of \$13,424,000 and has accounts receivable of \$2,684,400. What is Pick's accounts receivable turnover?

HP-38

Step	*Key in*	*Display shows*
1	13424000	13,424,000
2	↑	13,424,000.
3	2684400	2,684,400.
4	÷	5.00

Answer: 5.0

TI-MBA

Step	*Key in*	*Display shows*
1	13424000	13424000
2	÷	13424000
3	2684400	2684400
4	=	5.000745045

Answer: 5.0

Example 2 David Joseph Inc. has accounts receivable of \$5,395,000. If accounts receivable turnover for the year was 8.7, what were the company's sales for the year?

HP-38

Step	*Key in*	*Display shows*
1	5395000	5,395,000.
2	↑	5,395,000.00

Step	*Key in*	*Display shows*
3	8.7	8.7
4	×	46,936,500.00

Answer: $46,936,500

TI-MBA

Step	*Key in*	*Display shows*
1	5395000	5395000.
2	×	5395000.
3	8.7	8.7
4	=	46936500.

Answer: $46,936,500

AVERAGE INVENTORY TURNOVER

Because the amount in inventory changes over the course of time, the sales for that period can best be compared with that inventory when the average inventory is used. The average inventory is calculated, as you may have guessed by now, by adding the value of the inventory at the beginning of the year to the value of the inventory at the end of the year and dividing the result by 2.

The average inventory turnover is calculated by:

$$\frac{\text{Sales}}{\text{Average inventory}}$$

Once again cost of goods sold is often used in place of sales.

Example 1 Numeroff News began the current year with a total inventory of $3,500,000 and ended the year with inventory of $4,400,000. If sales for the year were $47,970,000, what is the average inventory turnover?

HP-38

Step	*Key in*	*Display shows*
1	3500000	3,500,000.
2	↑	3,500,000.00
3	4400000	4,400,000.
4	+	7.900,000.00
5	2	2.

Step	Key in	Display shows
6	÷	3,950,000.00
7	47970000	47,970,000.
8	x ≶ y	3,950,000.00
9	÷	12.14

Answer: 12.1

TI-MBA

Step	Key in	Display shows
1	3500000	3500000.
2	+	3500000.
3	4400000	4400000.
4	=	7900000.
5	÷	7900000.
6	2	2.
7	=	3950000.
8	STO 1	3950000.
9	47970000	47970000.
10	÷	47970000.
11	RCL 1	3950000.
12	=	12.1443038

Answer: 12.1

Example 2 Dolly Wen Industries began the year with inventory of \$1,750,000 and ended the year with inventory of \$2,356,000. If Dolly's average inventory turnover for the year was 12.3, what were their sales for the year?

HP-38

Step	Key in	Display shows
1	1750000	1,750,000.
2	↑	1,750,000.00
3	2356000	2,356,000.
4	+	4,106,000.00
5	12.3	12.3
6	X	50,503,800.00

Answer: \$50,503,800

TI-MBA

Step	Key in	Display shows
1	1750000	1750000.
2	+	1750000.
3	2356000	2356000.
4	=	4106000.
5	X	4106000.

Step	Key in	Display shows
6	12.3	12.3
7	=	50503800.

Answer: $50,503,800

Example 3 Microwave Manufacturers reports sales for the year of $3,456,000 and an ending inventory of $695,000. Find Microwave's inventory turnover.

HP-38

Step	Key in	Display shows
1	3456000	3,456,000.
2	↑	3,456,000.00
3	695000	695,000.
4	÷	4.97

Answer: 5.0

TI-MBA

Step	Key in	Display shows
1	3456000	3456000.
2	÷	3456000.
3	695000	695000.
4	=	4.972661871

Answer: 5.0

Example 4 The MicroLogic Corporation has an inventory of $3,995,000 and inventory turnover of 8.2. What is their annual sales?

HP-38

Step	Key in	Display shows
1	3995000	3,995,000.
2	↑	3,995,000.00
3	8.2	8.2
4	X	32,759,000.00

Answer: $32,759,000

TI-MBA

Step	Key in	Display shows
1	3995000	3995000.
2	X	3995000
3	8.2	8.2
4	=	32759000.

Answer: $32,759,000

ACCOUNTS RECEIVABLE TURNOVER

Most companies allow their customers to "buy now, pay later." The money owed to a company as a result of this plan is known as accounts receivable. Management of accounts receivable is another of the crucial elements in the success or failure of a commercial enterprise. While a company must allow its customers ample time to pay their debts, the firm should not be remiss in collecting debts that are overdue, or in taking as losses those debts that are deemed uncollectible. Therefore, the size of the accounts receivable should be held within reason. The reasonableness of a firm's accounts receivable is measured by the accounts receivable turnover, which is defined as:

$$\frac{\text{Sales}}{\text{Accounts receivable}}$$

It indicates how many times over the course of a year the average debt owed to a company is paid up.

AVERAGE ACCOUNTS RECEIVABLE TURNOVER

Since the value of accounts receivable changes over the course of a year, it is also common to compute accounts receivable turnover using the average accounts receivable. Average accounts receivable is calculated by adding the accounts receivable at the beginning of the year to that at the end of the year and dividing the result by 2 before dividing the total into sales for the year.

$$\text{Average accounts receivable turnover} = \frac{\text{Sales for year}}{(\text{Accounts receivable at start of year} + \text{accounts receivable at end of year}) \div 2}$$

Example 1 Benjamin Pick Corporation began the year with accounts receivable of \$2,854,000 and ended the year with accounts receivable of \$1,790,000. If sales for the year totaled \$28,999,000, what is Benjamin Pick's average accounts receivable turnover?

HP-38

Step	*Key in*	*Display shows*
1	28999000	28,999,000
2	↑	28,999,000.00
3	2854000	2,854,000.
4	↑	2,854,000.00
5	1790000	1,790,000.
6	+	4,644,000.00
7	2	2.
8	÷	2,322,000.00
9	÷	12.49

Answer: 12.49

TI-MBA

Step	*Key in*	*Display shows*
1	2854000	2854000.
2	+	2854000.
3	1790000	1790000.
4	=	4644000
5	÷	4644000.
6	2	2.
7	=	2322000.
8	STO 1	2322000.
9	28999000	28999000.
10	÷	28999000.
11	RCL 1	2322000
12	=	12.48880276

Answer: 12.49

Example 2 Hammer Associates had average accounts receivable of $322,000. If sales for the year were $3,850,900, what was the average accounts receivable turnover?

HP-38

Step	*Key in*	*Display shows*
1	3850900	3,850,900.
2	↑	3,850,900.00
3	322,000	322,000.
4	÷	11.96

Answer: 12.0

TI-MBA

Step	*Key in*	*Display shows*
1	3850900	3850900.
2	÷	3850900.

Step	*Key in*	*Display shows*
3	322000	322000.
4	=	11.95931677

Answer: 12.0

ACCOUNTS RECEIVABLE DAYS

To determine the average length of time a company's customers take to pay their debts, accounts receivable days, you only need to divide 365 by the accounts receivable turnover.

$$\text{Accounts receivable days} = \frac{365}{\text{Accounts receivable turnover}}$$

Example 1 Find the accounts receivable days for Benjamin Pick Corporation. (Refer to the previous section to get the average accounts receivable turnover.)

HP-38

Step	*Key in*	*Display shows*
1	365	365.
2	↑	365.00
3	12.49	12.49
4	÷	29.22

Answer: 29 days

TI-MBA

Step	*Key in*	*Display shows*
1	365	365.
2	↑	365.
3	12.49	12.49
4	=	29.2233787

Answer: 29 days

Example 2 Find the accounts receivable days for Hammer Associates.

HP-38

Step	*Key in*	*Display shows*
1	365	365.
2	↑	365.00

Step	*Key in*	*Display shows*
3	11.96	11.96
4	÷	30.52

Answer: 31 days

TI-MBA

Step	*Key in*	*Display shows*
1	365	365.
2	÷	365.
3	11.96	11.96
4	=	30.51839465

Answer: 31 days

OPERATING EXPENSE RATIO

The operating expense ratio defines management's ability to control expenses by determining what portion of sales is consumed by operating expenses. It is calculated by dividing operating expenses by sales.

$$\text{Operating expense ratio} = \frac{\text{Operating expenses}}{\text{Sales}}$$

Example 1 Bandler Buckles has sales of $1,575,000 and operating expenses of $1,322,917. Find their operating expense ratio.

HP-38

Step	*Key in*	*Display shows*
1	1322917	1,322,917.
2	↑	1,322,917.00
3	1575000	1,575,000.
4	÷	0.84

Answer: 84 percent

TI-MBA

Step	*Key in*	*Display shows*
1	1322917	1322917.
2	÷	1322917.
3	1575000	1575000
4	=	.8399473016.

Answer: 84 percent

Example 2 Brody Stones Inc. has sales of $655,387,000 and an operating expense ratio of 67 percent. Find their operating expenses.

HP-38

Step	*Key in*	*Display shows*
1	655387000	655,387,000.
2	↑	655,387,000.00
3	.67	0.67
4	×	439,109,290.00

Answer: $439,109,290

TI-MBA

Step	*Key in*	*Display shows*
1	655387000	655387000.
2	×	655387000.
3	.67	.67
4	=	439109290.

Answer: $439,109,290

INTEREST COVERAGE

A typical corporate income statement appears essentially as follows:

	Sales
less:	Cost of goods sold
	Gross profit
less:	Selling, general, and administrative expenses
	Earnings before interest and taxes (EBIT)
less:	Interest expense
	Earnings before taxes (EBT)
less:	Tax expense
	Profit after tax (PAT)

A corporation can protect itself from downturns in sales by reducing its expenses, thereby strengthening its profit level. For example, as sales decline the cost of goods sold (raw materials, labor, and other variable costs) correspondingly moves downward. Similarly, selling, general, and administrative expenses can be reduced by eliminating unnecessary staff or perhaps executive perquisites. Finally, if there is less income there will be correspondingly less tax expense. Virtually all a corporation's expenses may be reduced at its discretion except interest expense. Quite often interest expense is the money a corporation must pay to its bondholders for the continued use of their money. There may be thousands of such bondholders to whom the corporation is indebted. Consequently, it is almost impossible to renegotiate the terms of the bonds and reduce the interest expense. Moreover, if a company cannot meet the interest payments on its bonds, it may very likely be forced by its creditors into bankruptcy. Therefore it is of paramount importance that a ratio be constructed that measures a company's ability to meet its interest payments. Such a ratio measure is the interest coverage, which is defined as:

$$\frac{\text{Earnings before interest and taxes (EBIT)}}{\text{Interest expense}}$$

If a company has EBIT of $1,500,000 and interest expense of one million dollars the interest coverage is only 1.5, meaning that the money generated to cover interest cost is greater than the interest by only 50 percent. If EBIT were $5 million and interest expenses were still one million dollars, interest coverage would be 5.0, and the company would therefore be in a far stronger position to sustain a downturn.

Example 1 Herbert Cooper Industries has earnings before interest and taxes of $2,190,000 and interest expense of $1,500,000. Find their interest coverage.

HP-38

Step	*Key in*	*Display shows*
1	2190000	2,190,000.
2	↑	2,190,000.00
3	1500000	1,500,000.
4	÷	1.46

Answer: 1.5

TI-MBA

Step	*Key in*	*Display shows*
1	2190000	2190000.
2	÷	2190000.

Step	*Key in*	*Display shows*
3	1500000	1500000.
4	=	1.46

Answer: 1.5

Example 2 Mrs. Wilson's Pies has interest expense of $387,000 and interest coverage of 8.91. Find Mrs. Wilson's earnings before interest and taxes.

HP-38

Step	*Key in*	*Display shows*
1	387000	387,000.
2	↑	387,000.00
3	8.91	8.91
4	×	3,448,170.00

Answer: $3,448,170

TI-MBA

Step	*Key in*	*Display shows*
1	387000	387000.
2	×	387000
3	8.91	8.91
4	=	3448170.

Answer: $3,448,170

FIXED CHARGE COVERAGE

The idea behind the interest coverage ratio is to determine a company's ability to meet its fixed costs. In most companies, however, fixed costs are more than just interest expense. As a general rule fixed costs are taken to be interest expense plus one-third of the rent expense (the annual rent expense is usually available as a footnote to the financial statements). Therefore, the fixed charge coverage is calculated as:

$$\text{Fixed charge coverage} = \frac{\text{EBIT} + 1/3 \text{ Rent expense}}{\text{Interest expense} + 1/3 \text{ Rent expense}}$$

Example Dotson's Donuts has earnings before interest and taxes of $750,600 and rental expense of $125,000. If the interest expense is $222,000, what is the fixed charge coverage?

HP-38

Step	*Key in*	*Display shows*
1	125000	125,000.
2	↑	125,000.00
3	.33	.33
4	×	41,250.00
5	STO 1	41,250.00
6	750600	750,600
7	+	791,850.00
8	222000	222,000.
9	RCL 1	41,250.00
10	+	263,250.00
11	÷	3.01

Answer: 3.0

TI-MBA

Step	*Key in*	*Display shows*
1	125000	125000
2	×	125000.
3	.33	.33
4	=	41250.
5	STO 1	41250.
6	+	41250.
7	222000	222000.
8	=	263250.
9	STO 2	263250.
10	750600	750600.
11	+	750600.
12	RCL 1	41250.
13	=	791850.
14	÷	791850.
15	RCL 2	263250.
16	=	3.007977208

Answer: 3.0

INDEXING

It is frequently useful to compare a company's performance of one period to that of a prior period or a number of prior periods. While it is useful to glance at the actual numbers and attempt to glean an understanding from them, it is more helpful to put the numbers into perspective by translating them into similar terms through indexing.

Suppose a company had the following sales:

1976	$4,837,251
1977	$5,291,979
1978	$5,101,375
1979	$5,986,404
1980	$6,349,102

The discriminating eye can determine the path over which this company has traversed. For the rest of us the numbers are better understood when they are indexed, in other words, when they are all divided by a base figure, in this case, the sales of 1976. If this is done the figures become transformed into the following more understandable form:

1976	100
1977	109
1978	105
1979	124
1980	131

The reader of these numbers can quickly perceive the changes that have taken place in the business through the five-year period.

Indexing is particularly useful in situations where it is necessary to compare not just sales figures but entire income statements or balance sheets. Indexing enables the reader to evaluate at a glance what would otherwise be a complex series of numbers.

In almost every analysis of a company it is important to understand not only that company's performance but also the performance of its competitors. For this reason one should compare the ratios of a particular company with industry averages or those of other companies in the same industry.

Some ratios are more appropriate for particular types of businesses since they describe the key elements it takes to "make a buck" in that field. Therefore some of the ratios explained above should be given more weight in a specific analysis, while others should be ignored. It is up to your judgment as an analyst to discern which elements are crucial and hence which ratios to apply. It is not enough simply to calculate the ratios; that is only the first step. Once they are calculated, however, you will have the tools necessary to interpret a company's performance intelligently.

Finally, remember that no two businesses are alike. Sometimes you will come across situations that are totally different from those you have seen before. In such cases it may be necessary for you to create a new ratio that takes into account the crucial elements you believe make for success in that business.

SELF-TEST PROBLEMS

1. Below are the balance sheets and income statements for the year ended December 31, 1982. Study the sheets carefully and then find the information requested.

BUTTMAN PRODUCTS, INC. BALANCE SHEET

	For the Years Ended December 31,	
	1981	*1982*
Cash and Marketable Securities	$85,065	$92,560
Inventory	168,294	361,209
Accounts Receivable	522,123	604,320
Total Current Assets	$775,482	$1,058,089
Property, Plant, and Equipment	834,197	904,362
Other Assets	10,817	11,418
Total Assets	$1,620,496	$1,973,869
Current Liabilities	77,331	82,155
Long-Term Debt	508,930	731,717
Other Liabilities	89,421	89,421
Total Liabilities	$675,682	$903,293
Common Stock	100,000	100,000
Capital in Excess of Par Value	231,725	231,725
Retained Earnings	613,089	738,851
Total Shareholder's Equity	$944,814	$1,070,576
Total Liabilities of Shareholders' Equity	$1,620,496	$1,973,869

BUTTMAN PRODUCTS, INC. INCOME STATEMENT
YEAR ENDED DECEMBER 31, 1982

Sales	$2,135,000
Operating Expenses	1,387,500
Gross Profit	747,500
General and Administrative Expenses	300,102
Depreciation Expenses	114,875
Earnings before Interest and Taxes	$332,523
Interest Expense	$99,630
Income before Taxes	$232,893
Tax Expense	107,131
Net Income	$125,762

(a) Net profit margin
(b) Gross profit margin
(c) Return on equity
(d) Return on average equity
(e) Return on total assets
(f) Return on average assets
(g) Debt to total assets ratio
(h) Debt to equity ratio
(i) Long-term debt to total capitalization ratio
(j) Current ratio
(k) Quick ratio
(l) Inventory turnover
(m) Average inventory turnover
(n) Accounts receivable turnover
(o) Average accounts receivable turnover
(p) Accounts receivable days
(q) Operating expense ratio
(r) Interest coverage

2. Mitsumullish Company is an American trading concern with offices in 139 countries around the world. Every year the Benomian subsidiary earns at least 300 million Benomian nomas, the local currency. Often the subsidiary earns more than this amount, but rarely does it earn less. The currency trader at

Mitsumullish therefore feels comfortable in assuming that within three months' time she will have at least 300 million Benomian nomas to convert into American dollars. Currently there are 3529 Benomian nomas to the American dollar. However, there is a strong likelihood that within the following two months border skirmishes with Benomia's neighboring country Corbique will erupt into full-scale war. Such hostilities would have a devastating effect on the Benomian noma, vis-à-vis the American dollar. Accordingly, the currency trader at Mitsumullish would like to get a commitment from a purchaser of Benomian nomas for three months hence. This put will enable Mitsumullish to ensure that there will be a buyer for its nomas at the previously determined rate of 3529 Benomian nomas to the United States dollar.

If Mitsumullish's original investment in Benomia was 950,000 American dollars and the cost of the put is $26,500, what is its return on investment for the year?

(Hint: The cost of the put must be deducted from the profit before the return is calculated.)

CASE STUDY: LOMADE BROTHERS, INC.

"Hold all my calls Dorothy, I have to go over some important financial statements immediately, and I can't afford to be disturbed."

With that Len Grabbit closeted himself in his fifty-seventh-floor office at the headquarters office of Lomade Brothers, a prominent securities firm in the heart of New York's financial district. As he glanced down at the shimmering waters of the East River he noticed a helicopter lifting off from the Wall Street heliport. He wished he were inside that helicopter right now.

Len Grabbit graduated with a B.A. in economics from Eastern University in 1977. Upon graduation he joined Lomade Brothers as a financial analyst, where he has chalked up a run of enviable successes.

The previous Friday Len's boss, Joshua Tumblin, came rushing into Len's office and announced: "Len, I hate to mess up your weekend, but we have an emergency. You're probably aware that Tikva Incorporated is a large client of ours. We've just received a call from Dina Hewlett, their chief financial officer, telling us that they're a little upset over at Tikva at not being included in any of our monthly research notes. It sounds to me as though if we don't include them in the next issue we stand to lose their account. Len, we'd like you to produce an analysis of Tikva Inc. in time for the 5:00 P.M. deadline on Monday."

In his usual undaunted manner Len replied: "No problem, Josh, it shouldn't take me too long since I'm already familiar with the company."

Len asked his secretary Dorothy Meeskate to put a set of Tikva's most recent financial statements on his desk before she left for the weekend. These statements are in Exhibit 1.

The train that Len took home later that afternoon was delayed. He opened his briefcase and took out Tikva's financial statements. In glancing through them Len decided that Tikva had a great future. Over the past five years sales were up, gross profit was up, net profit was up, and total assets were growing at a fantastic rate. Len thought, "I'll put this in my briefcase till Monday morning. That will leave me plenty of time to write up an attractive blurb about Tikva."

Len arrived at his desk at 8:30 A. M. on Monday and immediately dictated his report on Tikva.

Dorothy typed up the memo and had it back on Len's desk at 9:45. Just as she left his office Rusty Leavitt, a fellow analyst at Lomade, knocked on Len's door. He entered and, walking up to Len's desk, noticed the name Tikva on a sheet of paper.

"Oh, I see you're looking at Tikva. I spent a little time on their financial statements last week. What a dog! It looks like the company's going to hell in a basket."

"I don't know what you mean," Len retorted. "Prospects for Tikva look pretty good to me. After all, for each of the past five years sales are up, gross profit is up, net profit is up, and total assets are up. I've just written a memo for this month's research notes describing Tikva's sunny future.

"You'd better come over to my office right away, Len," Rusty suggested.

Rusty pulled out a sheet of paper filled with ratios and other data relating to Tikva Inc. (see Exhibit 2).

"Here's the situation as I see it, Len. You're right about sales being up, but gross profit and net profit aren't up nearly as much. You can see that in the first three lines on the sheet. Those lines are an index of the three items as they appear on Tikva's income statement. What's more, it's taken an increasingly large amount of total assets to generate that profit. That's the good news. The bad news is that in each of the past five years net profit margin is down, gross profit margin is down, return on equity is down, return on assets is down, interest coverage is down, accounts receivable turnover is down, and the firm has had to borrow increasing amounts of money to finance assets that are growing as fast as rabbits."

"Slow down, slow down, Leavitt. Let me borrow that sheet. I'll return it to you at 5:05 today." With that Len returned somewhat shaken to his office.

What would you do?

EXHIBIT 1 TIKVA INCORPORATED BALANCE SHEET FOR THE YEARS ENDING DECEMBER 31

	1982	*1981*	*1980*	*1979*	*1978*
Assets:					
Cash	$86,967	$77,649	$69,329	$61,901	$55,268
Marketable Securities	3,000	7,000	8,000	6,000	5,000
Accounts Receivable	817,487	667,780	540,769	458,069	384,947
Inventory	955,529	791,513	653,705	552,115	464,715
Total Current Assets	$1,862,983	$1,543,942	$1,271,803	$1,107,785	$909,930
Property, Plant, and Equipment	300,000	300,000	300,000	300,000	300,000
Less: Accumulated Depreciation	(140,000)	(130,000)	(120,000)	(110,000)	(100,000)
Total Assets	$2,022,983	$1,713,942	$1,451,803	$1,297,785	$1,109,930
Liabilities:					
Accounts Payable	$97,251	$97,522	$98,159	$98,749	$98,493
Notes Payable	101,221	101,502	102,165	102,780	102,513
Total Current Liabilities	$198,472	$199,024	$200,324	$201,529	$201,006
Long-Term Debt	$705,016	$475,600	$291,363	$213,788	$103,213
Total Liabilities	$903,488	$674,624	$491,687	$415,317	$304,219
Common Stock	200,000	200,000	200,000	200,000	200,000
Paid-In Capital	300,000	300,000	300,000	300,000	300,000
Retained Earnings	619,495	539,318	460,116	382,468	305,711
Total Shareholders' Equity and Liabilities	$2,022,983	$1,713,942	$1,451,803	$1,297,785	$1,109,930

STATEMENTS OF INCOME FOR THE YEARS ENDING DECEMBER 31,

	1982	1981	1980	1979	1978
Net Sales	$1,739,334	$1,552,977	$1,386,586	$1,238,024	$1,105,378
Cost of Goods Sold	1,234,927	1,071,554	915,147	779,955	663,227
Gross Profit	$504,407	$481,423	$471,439	$458,069	$442,151
Selling, General, and Administrative Expenses	$263,709	$261,197	$269,331	$264,104	$260,146
Depreciation Expenses	10,000	10,000	10,000	10,000	10,000
Earnings before Interest and Taxes	$230,698	$210,226	$192,108	$183,965	$172,005
Interest Expense	56,401	38,048	23,309	17,103	8,257
Profit before Taxes	$174,298	$172,178	$168,800	$166,863	$163,748
Tax Expense	94,121	92,976	91,152	90,106	88,424
Profit after Taxes	$80,177	$79,202	$77,648	$76,757	$75,324

EXHIBIT 2 ANALYSIS OF TIKVA INC.

	1982	1981	1980	1979	1978
Sales	157	140	125	112	100
Gross Profit	114	109	107	104	100
Net Profit	106	105	103	102	100
Total Assets	182	154	131	117	100
Net Profit Margin	4.6%	5.1%	5.6%	6.2%	6.8%
Gross Profit Margin	29.0%	31.0%	34.0%	37.0%	38.2%
Return on Equity	7.2%	7.6%	8.1%	8.7%	9.3%
Return on Average Equity	7.4%	7.9%	8.4%	9.1%	n/a
Return on Total Assets	4.0%	4.6%	5.3%	5.9%	6.8%
Return on Average Assets	4.3%	5.0%	5.6%	6.4%	n/a
Interest Coverage	4.1x	5.5x	8.2x	10.8x	20.8x
Debt/Total Assets	44.7%	39.4%	33.9%	32.0%	27.4%
Debt: Equity	1:1.2	1:1.5	1:2	1:2.1	1:2.6
Long-Term Debt/Total Capitalization	38.6%	31.4%	23.3%	19.5%	11.4%
Current Ratio	9.4x	7.8x	6.3x	5.5x	4.5x
Quick Ratio	4.6x	3.8x	3.1x	2.8x	2.2x
Inventory Turnover (COGS)	1.3x	1.4x	1.4x	1.4x	1.4x
Average Inventory Turnover	1.4x	1.5x	1.5x	1.5x	n/a
Accounts Receivable Turnover	2.1x	2.3x	2.6x	2.7x	2.9x
Average Turnover	2.3x	2.6x	2.8x	2.9x	n/a
Accounts Receivable Days	174	159	140	135	126

Note: n/a = not available

Alternative Solutions Both Rusty Leavitt and Len Grabbit are correct. As Len claimed, gross profits are up, net profits are up, and total assets are growing. However, Rusty's counterarguments have merit, too. In fact, over the previous five years the company has indeed increased its profit, but it has done so only by increasing its investment and its debt. On an absolute basis it is encouraging to note that the firm is making increasing amounts of money. Yet, it is disappointing to find that such increases have been made possible by injections of funds from debt and equity sources.

As an investor, one should be most concerned about the deterioration of Tikva's profitability rates. Accordingly, we feel that Len Grabbit should issue strong words of caution in Tikva's monthly research notes to actual and potential investors.

The answers do not come from numbers alone. Almost every large company has a department known as the Public Relations Department, the Shareholder Relations Department, the Investor Relations Department, or a similar title. Len would be well advised to phone Tikva's Public Relations Department and ask for an explanation behind the decline in Tikva's profitability ratios. In fact, any small investor can make this kind of inquiry; such displays of interest are usually well received by a company. (Of course, it is often in the company's interest to paint as rosy a picture as possible, but when the company's explanation is viewed in conjunction with the related financial ratios, a clearer picture of the company's activities will generally emerge.)

7 Depreciation

Most corporations must make large expenditures to buy large tangible assets. Such purchases are necessary in the normal course of business and are not recorded as expenses; they are merely the transfer of assets from one form to another. For example, if General Motors builds a new manufacturing plant for $100 million, it will simply have transferred $100 million of cash into $100 million of fixed assets, in this case "Property, Plant, and Equipment."

The life of most fixed assets is finite. The amount expended to make their purchase is effectively consumed over the life of the asset. Therefore, generally accepted accounting principles and the Internal Revenue Service allow a company to deduct from its annual income a portion of the cost of its fixed assets. Such deductions are known as *depreciation* and are designed to encourage a firm to build a reserve with which it can acquire new assets when the life of the existing assets expires.

There are three generally accepted methods of accounting for depreciation. To illustrate all three types we shall examine a case in which a company buys an asset for $20,000. The company's engineers estimate that the asset will last for 15 years; after that period it can be sold for scrap value of $5,000. The depreciable value is therefore $15,000 (cost value of $20,000 less salvage value of $5,000).

STRAIGHT-LINE METHOD

The straight-line method of depreciation states that the company may deduct from its income an equal amount each year, over the life of the asset. In the above example the depreciation per year is $1,000 ($15,000 divided by 15 years, the estimated useful life of the asset) or 6.66 percent per year.

DOUBLE DECLINING BALANCE METHOD

The double declining balance method allows a company to take twice (hence the name *double*) the percentage of annual depreciation expense as the straight-line method permits. However, under the double declining balance method the percentage is taken of the current book value of the asset. The book value of the asset is reduced each year by the amount of depreciation taken that year. In contrast to the straight-line method in the double declining balance method the salvage value is not deducted from the cost in calculating the depreciable value. Rather, the cost is used as the depreciable value. The asset is depreciated until the book value reaches $5000 (the salvage value). This usually happens before the estimated life of the asset expires. For the above example, the double declining balance method dictates the following depreciation schedule.

Year	*Annual Depreciation Expense*	*Accumulated Depreciation*	*Book Value of Asset*
1	2,667	2,667	17,333
2	2,311	4,978	15,022
3	2,003	6,981	13,019
4	1,736	8,717	11,283
5	1,504	10,221	9,779
6	1,304	11,525	8,475
7	1,130	12,655	7,345
8	979	13,634	6,366
9	849	14,483	5,517
10	517	15,000	5,000
11	—0—	15,000	5,000
12	—0—	15,000	5,000

Year	Annual Depreciation Expense	Accumulated Depreciation	Book Value of Asset
13	—0—	15,000	5,000
14	—0—	15,000	5,000
15	—0—	15,000	5,000

SUM OF THE YEARS DIGITS METHOD

If we were to take the column labeled "Year" in the above table and add together all the numbers in that column, they would total 120. Such an addition is, in fact, performed in the sum of the years digits method, and the first year's depreciation percentage is the number of the last year divided by the sum of the years. In our example the first year's depreciation is equal to:

$$\frac{15}{120} \times 15{,}000 = \$1{,}875$$

Note that under this method the depreciable value is equal to the cost minus the salvage value, as in the straight-line method.

The following table describes how the sum of the years digits method is used based on our example.

Year	Ratio	Annual Depreciation Expense	Accumulated Depreciation	Book Value of Asset
1	15/120	1,875	1,875	18,125
2	14/120	1,750	3,625	16,375
3	13/120	1,625	5,250	14,750
4	12/120	1,500	6,750	13,250
5	11/120	1,375	8,125	11,875
6	10/120	1,250	9,375	10,625
7	9/120	1,125	10,500	9,500
8	8/120	1,000	11,500	8,500
9	7/120	875	12,375	7,625
10	6/120	750	13,125	6,875
11	5/120	625	13,750	6,250
12	4/120	500	14,250	5,750
13	3/120	375	14,625	5,375

Year	Ratio	Annual Depreciation Expense	Accumulated Depreciation	Book Value of Asset
14	2/120	250	14,875	5,125
15	1/120	125	15,000	5,000

As you have probably noticed, both the double declining balance and the sum of the year's digits method allow a company to deduct larger amounts of depreciation in the early years of the asset's life than the straight-line method. The object of such accelerated depreciation is to offset a greater amount of income in the earlier years so that the amount of taxable income is reduced, resulting in a smaller tax bill.

If a company has an especially handsome net income in a particular year, it would probably prefer to use an accelerated depreciation method for assets acquired that year. Conversely, if net income is down for the year, the corporate executives will probably want to give the shareholders as rosy a picture as possible and opt for the straight-line method. The method selected is at the discretion of the company.

SELF-TEST PROBLEMS

1. Radin Industries buys a new computer for $137,500. They estimate that the computer will have a useful life of 15 years and a salvage value of $10,000. Calculate the depreciation rate for each of the 15 years using:

   (a) Straight-line method
   (b) Double declining balance method
   (c) Sum of the years digits method

2. Sullivan Industries buys some heavy tanks for an expansion of their refining business at a cost of $798,000. They believe that after 12 years the tanks will have a salvage value of $17,500. Calculate the rate of depreciation for each of the 12 years using each of the three depreciation methods.

CASE STUDY: THE ADAM COMPUTER COMPANY

The Adam Computer Company was formed recently. Although still young the company has experienced rapid growth in line with that of its industry—home computers. The latest projections for the industry's growth show that the sales in the next four years will increase only slightly, but in the fifth year they will accelerate sharply.

In light of these projections top management of the company was heavily involved in planning to add capacity to its existing manufacturing facility in Waco, Texas.

As a first step toward expension Adam Computer planned the purchase and construction of a prefabricated building to house a future factory in the heart of industrial Waco. The cost of the proposed building was $175,000 and the manufacturer's engineers estimated that at the end of 15 years the remains of the building could be sold for $25,000.

Management at Adam had decided that the purchase of this building was an appropriate step. Once the decision had been made, the discussion focused on whether to depreciate the proposed factory on a straight-line or accelerated method. However, since profit was expected to balloon in five years, it was pointed out that it would be desirable to have a similar ballooning of depreciation expense to lighten the tax burden on the firm.

Claude Pinkerton, controller of Adam, advocated the use of the straight-line method, since he felt it was futile to adopt any other method in attempting to offset future income. He believed that the date at which income would greatly expand was sufficiently vague to mitigate any effort at tax reduction.

Pascal Chiroc, chief accountant at Adam, was the major proponent for adopting an accelerated method. While he admitted that the exact timing of any future burst in income was unclear, he maintained that in any event income would be greater in the first half of the asset's life than in second half.

The following list describes the depreciation expense under each of the three possible methods.

Year	Straight-Line	Double Declining Balance	Sum of the Years Digits
1	10,000	$23,333	$18,750
2	10,000	20,222	17,500
3	10,000	17,526	16,250
4	10,000	15,189	15,000
5	10,000	13,164	13,750
6	10,000	11,409	12,500
7	10,000	9,888	11,250
8	10,000	8,569	10,000
9	10,000	7,426	8,750
10	10,000	6,437	7,500
11	10,000	5,579	6,250
12	10,000	4,834	5,000
13	10,000	4,189	3,750
14	10,000	2,235	2,500
15	10,000	—0—	1,250

What would you do?

Recommended Solution Since all the calculations necessary for the solution of this problem have already been made and exhibited in the list, the remaining issues are qualitative.

We feel that the goal of the company in choosing a depreciation rate is to maximize the depreciation expense in year 5. Accordingly, we chose the sum of the years digits method, because it has the greatest depreciation expense in the fifth year.

8 Modern Portfolio Theory

There are two major avenues through which a company may obtain capital. The first source is debt, which includes any type of borrowing the company may engage in. The second source is equity, which involves investment in the company by shareholders and includes the profit generated from such investment.

It is essential to be aware of the cost of capital in an investment *before* the investment is made. An investor who is unaware of the cost of capital is analogous to a shopper who buys an entire wardrobe without asking its price. We will return to this issue of cost of capital shortly.

BETA COEFFICIENTS

The price of almost every stock moves in conjunction with the overall market trend. That is, if the stock market as a whole is moving upward the odds are that any given stock will increase in price as well. Conversely, a downward moving market would tend to depress the price of a particular stock.

Although most stocks follow market trends, they do so in varying degrees. If the market overall moves up 10 percent and a particular stock climbs 10 percent, that stock is said to have a beta coefficient of 1.0. If the market moves up 10 percent and a particular stock climbs only 8 percent that stock has a beta coefficient of 0.8, since the change in its value is 80 percent of the change in the market value. If a stock has a beta coefficient of 1.2 it is expected to move up 120 percent if the market rises 10 percent.

It would seem from this description that every investor would want to buy only those stocks with high beta coefficients. The drawback to such a strategy is that, just as high beta coefficient stocks move up more than the market when the market rises, so too they move down more than the market when the market declines. Beta coefficients are usually calculated by a computer, using an elaborate and complex formula based on the past performance of the stocks.

RISK-FREE RATE

Every investment entails a certain degree of risk. Generally the more risky a potential investment as compared to the overall market of investments, the greater the return will be. Of course, the less risky a venture as compared to the overall market, the less will its return be. The most safe investments are referred to as being risk-free although they are in truth not free of *all* risk; when compared with all other potential investments they are *relatively* risk-free. In modern times the typical risk-free investments are United States Treasury notes and bonds, obligations of the federal government of the United States. Since the United States is regarded as the richest and most stable government in the world its obligations are the most likely to be honored.

The risk-free rate is constantly in flux because of changes in interest rates, which are based on many factors.

RETURN ON THE OVERALL MARKET

The combination of all returns offered by every investment available to investors is the return on the overall market. If a firm offering an investment wishes to offer a return different than the return on the overall market, be it greater or less than the market's return, the potential investment must entail a different degree of risk than the overall market risk.

As you may have guessed, the return on the overall market is not a single number, and there is no simple or even complex formula from which to calculate it. At best it can be estimated, and many securities firms offer their services (including their computers) in making such an estimation. Usually the return on the overall market is arrived at through the prior construction of a *security market line* (SML). The SML is a graph that depicts the return on an investment given its beta coefficient, as in the following example.

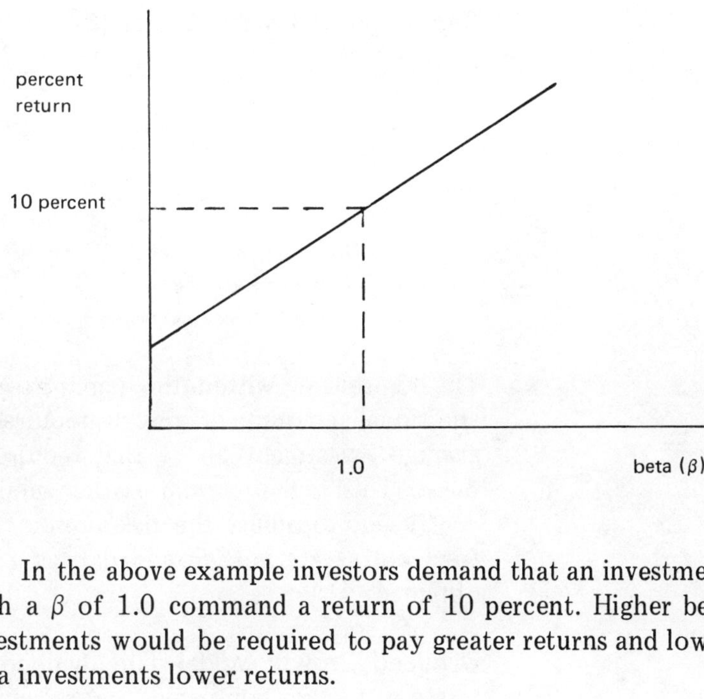

In the above example investors demand that an investment with a β of 1.0 command a return of 10 percent. Higher beta investments would be required to pay greater returns and lower beta investments lower returns.

COST OF CAPITAL

The cost of capital to a company has two components: the cost of debt and the cost of equity.

The cost of debt is simply the interest expense divided by the debt of the company. For example, if a company has $100,000 of annual interest expense and one million dollars of debt, its pretax cost of debt is 10 percent. Assuming a 50 percent tax rate, the after-tax cost of debt is 5 percent.

$$\frac{\$100,000}{\$1,000,000} \times 50 \text{ percent} = 5 \text{ percent}$$

There are a number of ways to calculate the cost of equity, the second of the two components in a firm's capitalization. We shall discuss the capital asset pricing model and the divided growth model.

Capital Asset Pricing Model (CAPM) The formula for calculating CAPM is:

$$\text{CAPM} = R_F + \beta (R_M - R_F)$$

where

R_F = risk-free rate
β = beta coefficient
R_M = return on the overall market

The expression within the parentheses (R_M - R_F) gives the additional amount of return required by investors for the average investment above that required for a risk-free investment. This *risk premium* is then multiplied by a firm's beta coefficient to adjust the risk premium to that firm. The risk-free return rate is then added back in and the cost of equity obtained.

Dividend Growth Model The dividend growth model is appropriate to use for companies that are currently paying dividends. The model states that the cost of equity is equal to the dividend yield plus expected growth in the dividend yield. The computation of such growth is a subjective matter. However, there are several common ways of calculating such growth.

First, past growth of dividends over the recent past; second, the growth rate of earnings per share in the recent past; and last, the growth rate of net earnings.

Once you have calculated the cost of debt and the cost of equity, you are ready to calculate the company's cost of capital. Normally the *weighted-average cost of capital* is computed. The weighted-average cost of capital takes into account the structure of a firm's financing. The after-tax cost of debt is multiplied by the percentage of capitalization that debt represents (this percentage is the now familiar debt/total assets ratio). Then the cost of equity is multiplied by the percent of capitalization that equity represents. That percentage is 1 - (debt ÷ total assets). Finally, the weighted average cost of debt and the weighted average cost of equity and the cost of capital are obtained.

INVESTMENT OPPORTUNITIES

Among the great strengths of the capitalist system is its ability to allow its constituents to obtain the goods they desire. Since capital is necessary for almost every enterprise, a true capitalist system has a myriad of investment forms for funneling capital to various investment vehicles. In this chapter we will describe the benefits and drawbacks of some of the more popular investment opportunities.

Every investor is different. A young couple in their early thirties, with a house and a large mortgage, have different investment needs from a teenager with a summer job, or a retiree with a large estate. There are, however, similarities among all investors. In almost every case it is unwise to invest all one's funds in a single venture. Since no investment is absolutely foolproof, the risk of a single investment can be reduced by diversifying a portfolio. Almost every portfolio is constructed like a pyramid, with a large portion of the portfolio invested in relatively safer investments as a firm foundation, and an ever-decreasing amount in increasingly riskier enterprises. The dimensions of the pyramid will, of course, vary from investor to investor as strategies implying a different preference for risk are selected. Some investors need absolute certainty that their principal will be returned, while others can afford to place their entire investment at risk on the chance that they may receive an extremely high return. Generally, the greater the risk the higher the potential return and the greater the possibility for total loss. A portfolio should, therefore, be a *combination* of various securities and investment opportunities.

INTEREST RATES

The only thing constant about interest rates is that they are always changing. Every time a security is traded the price of that security implies a perception of the current interest rate structure. For example, if an investor paid $1000 for a bond of XYZ Company that will pay her $40 every six months and return her $1000 at the end of seven years, the investor perceived at the time that she was appropriately compensated for the risk involved, at a rate of 8 percent per year.

The rate of interest an investor can expect to receive from a security is based on the risk involved in that security (whether the interest and principal repayments will be made) and the general level of interest rates. That general level is determined by many factors. For an investor to receive a real return, the interest rate received must be greater than the inflation rate. In other words, if inflation is 10 percent per year, and the rate of return is only 8 percent, the value of the investor's original principal is decreasing at the rate of 10 percent per year while he or she is receiving only 8 percent per year. Instead of gaining, the investor's principal has decreased in value by 2 percent per year. Therefore, interest rates must be above that of inflation to generate investor interest.

Over the past few years the rate of inflation has been exceedingly high by historical standards. Accordingly, inflation has played a large role in determining the general level of interest rates. If the collective wisdom of all the players in the market is of the opinion that inflation will rise in a year, then securities with a maturity of greater than one year will have to pay a substantially higher interest rate than securities with a maturity of less than one year. If most people believe that inflation will go down in a year then short-term securities will have to pay a higher rate than long-term securities to assure the investor of a "real" return. Under "normal" circumstances, where inflation is expected to remain constant, long-term securities usually pay a higher rate of interest since investors put their money at risk for a greater length of time.

The general level of interest rates is determined by an infinite number of variables. In addition to inflation, the number of potential borrowers and lenders in the market is said to have a large influence. The other factors that influence interest rates are so vast, varied, complex, and yet subtle that no single person could name them all. Everything from the weather in Trinidad to disturbances on the surface of the sun are said to exert some influence on interest rates.

SAVINGS BANKS

Americans have always placed very high emphasis on the goal of owning their own homes. More than any others, the savings and loan associations have been the financial intermediaries that have facilitated the private ownership of millions of residences, by accepting deposits and lending out these same funds to purchasers of homes.

Historically, the deposits in a savings and loan association were of short duration. Depositors always had the opportunity to withdraw their funds at any time. Conversely, the mortgage loans made by the bank were long term. As mentioned above, long-term interest rates are higher than short-term interest rates, so the banks lent money at long-term rates and kept the "spread" for profit. The depositors received their interest, the borrowers bought their homes, and the banks earned their profits; a great deal all around.

In recent years inflation has caused interest rates to skyrocket. Savings and loan associations, however, were prevented from increasing the interest paid to depositors by two factors:

1. Regulation Q, a rule of the federal government, places a ceiling on the rate of interest that a bank may pay its depositors.
2. Most savings and loan associations were locked into mortgage loans at low rates of interest.

Regulation Q is being phased out by statutory measures. The second factor, however, is not as easily rectified. In the past banks held short-term deposits and long-term loans. They made money only because interest rates experienced very little fluctuation. Once interest rates became more volatile it became necessary for banks to make long-term loans only from money received from depositors on a long-term basis. Hence, in recent years, various types of deposits have proliferated at savings and loan associations. Among the new types of deposits are those for periods of six months, one year, and two and a half years, whose interest rates are directly linked to those of government-issued securities of a similar maturity. There is, however, a subtle difference between government securities and those issued by banks.

GOVERNMENT SECURITIES

Six-month Treasury bills (T-bills) have a face value of $10,000; that is, six months from the original date of purchase, the government will pay the holder of the bill $10,000. The original purchaser of the bill pays an amount something less than $10,000, the difference representing the interest earned. If a six-month treasury bill is originally purchased for $9,500 it is said to have been discounted by 10 percent, since the $500 discount is 5 percent of $10,000 and the time period involved is only half a year rather than a whole year. The purchaser of such a T-bill invests $9,500 and receives $500 in interest after the next six months. Since

$$\frac{500}{9500} = 5.3 \text{ percent}$$

giving an annual yield of 10.6 percent, the purchaser of the T-bill receives an effective yield of 10.6 percent on a Treasury bill that was discounted by 10 percent. Savings banks that issue securities linked to rates on Treasury instruments use the discount rate and *not* the yield rate in determining the interest to be paid to the investor. Therefore, investors considering the purchase of a savings certificate from a bank would be wise to consider an alternate investment in Treasury securities. Six-month Treasury bills are sold every Monday at the various Federal Reserve banks around the country. Individuals can go to the Federal Reserve bank in their area with $10,000 and purchase a Treasury instrument. The Treasury takes the $10,000 and after the discount rate for the week is determined (at an auction of large-denomination Treasury securities), the Treasury sends a certificate and the appropriate amount of money (the discount) to the investor. If this is too much of an inconvenience, most stockbrokers will purchase a Treasury bill for you, but they will probably charge a commission. After Treasury instruments have been purchased for the first time, they are often bought and sold before maturity in what is known as the aftermarket. Therefore, if an investor wants to buy a Treasury security for a period of, say, only two weeks, it may be purchased in the aftermarket.

Many financial institutions pay higher interest rates for deposits of larger amounts. These securities are often known as CDs or certificates of deposit. To avail themselves of these high rates, small investors pool their funds in what are known as money market funds. The proliferation of money market funds in recent years has led to the availability of high-yield opportunities with low risk for small investors.

BONDS

Corporate Bonds To grow and prosper, corporations often construct new facilities, such as factories. In many instances the company needs to borrow the money to build its plant, since the cost often runs into the tens of millions of dollars and most companies do not keep that kind of money around in petty cash. If the company intends to repay the money within a short time, it can usually go to its commercial banker, who is able to arrange a short-term loan (generally less than ten years). If the amount of money requested is too large for any single bank to make the loan, the company's banker can arrange a syndicate of banks who will each lend the company a portion of the funds desired.

A company can also decide that it wants to match the life of the loan to the life of the asset. (This is a very commonplace decision and is congruent to the "matching" principle of the financial accounting world.) Accordingly, the loan is taken out and repaid over the life of the asset. If the plant to be built is expected to last for 20 years, the company will want to take out a loan for that number of years. Since it is not normal practice for a commercial bank to lend money to a business for such a great length of time, the company is forced to go elsewhere to obtain the funds. At this time the company makes its appearance in the capital markets. First, the company orders several thousand documents from its printer that state that each holder of these papers is entitled to receive $1000 at the end of the loan, and an appropriate rate of interest each year until maturity. The company calls such pieces of paper *bonds* and sells them to the general public. In this manner the small investor has an opportunity to act as banker, and the company gets the money it needs. The capital market is composed of thousands of such bonds, and investors have many opportunities to "rent" their funds to the most attractive borrower. Often when the bond reaches maturity the company that borrowed the money does not have the funds to repay what it originally borrowed. Such companies usually issue new bonds to pay off the old ones; this is known in the financial world as "rolling over" old debt.

The interest individuals receive from the corporate bonds they own is taxable income and is reported to the Internal Revenue Service by the company that pays the interest, just as the company must report its employees' salaries to the IRS. But if an individual is already earning a salary that puts him or her in a 50-percent tax bracket, then after taxes he or she will wind up with only half of the interest payments from the company. This has resulted in the advent of the "tax-free" bond. Usually issued by a governmental agency, such bonds are exempt from federal income taxes (they are usually not exempt from state taxes), so that high tax bracket investors can invest their funds without having to pay anything to the IRS. For an investor in a 50-percent tax bracket, this *doubles* the value of the investment. Since the organizations that issue tax-free bonds are also financially wise, they will not pay as much interest on their bonds as a company that issues taxable bonds. Usually, the interest rates on tax-free bonds are a little more than half those on comparable corporate bonds.

Government Bonds To finance its deficit, the federal government of the United States also issues bonds. The bonds of the government are *not* tax exempt, despite the fact that they are issued by a government agency. While this distinction may appear at first glance to be an oversight, there is nonetheless good reason for the bonds of the federal government to be subject to taxation.

The rate of return on an investment depends on the level of risk involved in it. Since the government of the United States is regarded as the most secure and stable in the world, the securities it issues are also held in the highest esteem; there can be no investment safer than an investment in instruments of the United States federal government. If the federal government were to issue nontaxable bonds, the other bonds in the nontaxable arena could not compete in terms of risk and would therefore be unable to attract any investors. To allow other governmental agencies to attract investor interest, the federal government issues only taxable securities.

Rating Agencies Many investors are confused by the large number of investment opportunities in the bond market. They find it difficult to distinguish among the various bonds. For this reason, there are companies called rating agencies; the best known are Moody's and Standard & Poors. These companies study the issuers of bonds and rate them according to the likelihood that the bonds will be paid off at maturity and that interest payments will be made in the interim. Over the past few years new rating agencies have come to the fore to challenge the supremacy of Moody's and Standard & Poors, but the two leading firms have entrenched themselves over many years, and any challenge to their leadership will be a tough, uphill battle.

STOCKS

The stockholders of a company are the company's owners. Thousands of companies have shares that are traded on public exchanges (such as the New York Stock Exchange, the American Stock Exchange, the Pacific Stock Exchange, to name a few) and the owners of a company can buy or sell their holdings at almost any time through one of these exchanges. The existence of stock exchanges has facilitated wide distribution of shareholdings in the United States.

Even the shares of those companies not listed on a stock exchange can be traded publicly. This is accomplished through the "over-the-counter" market. Numerous firms in the securities industry announce that they will be "making a market" in a particular security. When that occurs all orders to buy or sell that security are channeled by other brokerage houses to the firm that is "making the market." The buy and sell orders meet, and when there is a buy order with a sell order at a corresponding price the orders are both executed.

There are different kinds of stocks, and it is not fair to say that one stock is good for every investor. Most experienced investors have a portfolio composed of many stocks. At one end of the spectrum are the utility companies. Most utilities have their rates (and hence their income) determined in advance by a rate-setting commission at a governmental level. Therefore, the stocks of utilities usually do not move up or down very much and are not too exciting. However, their performance can be relied upon to a greater extent than those of most other companies, and they usually pay high dividends. Investors who buy stocks of utility companies are usually looking for a high rate of return, along with a high degree of certainty that their original investment will be returned.

Utilities often issue "preferred" stock in addition to the "common" stock that all publicly held companies sell. Preferred stock is a hybrid security in that it is half-bond, half-stock. It is a stock because it represents ownership in the company. However, in case a company files bankruptcy or goes out of business, the preferred shareholders have a higher priority in receiving funds when the company's assets are liquidated. Also, preferred stock almost always has a prestated dividend rate, which is higher than that of the common shares, and if the preferred shares are "cumulative" the company is allowed to omit a dividend only if it makes up that dividend in a later year. Also, most companies are not permitted to pay dividends to common shareholders if dividends to preferred shareholders are in arrears. However, preferred shareholders generally do not share in the profits of a corporation past the extent of their dividends.

At the other end of the spectrum are high-risk stocks. The price of these stocks usually fluctuates greatly, and consequently they entail a great degree of risk. More often than not these companies' stocks do not pay any dividend, as the return to the shareholders is expected to come from appreciation in the value of the shares. In recent years the major industry whose stocks are considered high risk has been high technology, where major breakthroughs occur suddenly and unexpectedly and yield great rewards. There is an almost infinite variety of stocks between these two extremes.

Selling Short Almost everybody knows that if investors believe a stock price will go up they should buy the stock and if they believe that a stock price will go down, they should sell the stock. The constant fluctuation of stock prices indicates the state of flux that the combined wisdom of all investors represents. There are times, however, when an investor may believe that a stock price will go down but she does not own any of the stock. Since everyone knows that you cannot sell what you do not own, it would seem impossible for the investor to take advantage of her insight.

Enter the investor's broker. Almost every brokerage firm will allow customers to sell a stock "short," that is, to sell shares of a company that they do not own. Investors "sell short" when they believe that the price of a share of stock will be going down. The brokerage firm effectively lends the shares of stock to the investor and the investor sells them. Investors are free to repurchase the shares of stock in the open market to repay their brokers. Such repayment must normally occur within 30 days of the short sale. If the price of the stock has moved down in the interim, the investor repays the broker with shares bought at a lower price. If the price has moved up in a 30-day period, the investor has to repay the broker with shares that are more expensive than the ones sold. Normally, the investor must forward to the broker half the value of the shares sold short at the time of the short sale. This provides the broker with a degree of confidence that the investor can muster the funds necessary to pay the broker. If the price of the shares moves up while the investor is in a "short" position, the broker usually asks for more money, since many brokerage firms have a rule that half the value of the shares sold short must always be on deposit with the firm.

Buying in Lots It is often advantageous for an investor to purchase stock in excess of 100 shares at a time. For purchases of less than 100 shares, brokers often add an extra fee to conduct the transaction, generally around one-eighth to one-half a point per share. One hundred shares is called a "round-lot"; fewer than 100 shares is called an "odd-lot."

Choosing a Broker Before 1975 all brokerage firms were forced by regulation of the Securities and Exchange Commission to charge the same brokerage rates. Since May 1, 1975 (often referred to as the Mayday of the securities industry), brokers have been free to set their own rates. As a result, a two-tiered structure has evolved within the brokerage industry. Generally speaking, investors can choose between two types of brokerage firms: full-service and discount brokerage. A full-service firm such as Merrill Lynch, Shearson/American Express, or E. F. Hutton will offer investors the advice of a broker and a full spectrum of research on companies to invest in, as well as other financial advice. Discount brokerage firms offer no such amenities, nor do they provide a broker with whom the investor may commiserate. However, the fees charged by discount brokerage houses are considerably less than those charged by full-service firms. For investors who rely on their own research to make their investments, the discount firm is probably most advantageous. For those who prefer to discuss the matter with a professional the full-service firm is often the best.

Buying on Margin Almost all brokerage firms will allow their clients to buy stock "on margin." Buying on margin allows investors to pay only half the value of the stock they are buying. The other half is effectively borrowed from the brokerage firm. The interest rate varies with the general interest rate level and is usually dependent upon the broker-loan rate (the interest rate at which major banks will lend money to large brokerage houses). The advantage of buying on margin is that investors can get double the buying power. If the stock moves up, investors get double the profits they would get if they had bought only half the stock. However, if the stock moves down they suffer double the losses. In both cases the cost of borrowing the money from the brokerage firm must be deducted before net profit is calculated. When buying on margin it is usually wise to be very confident that the stock being purchased will increase in value. Taking losses on a stock bought on margin can be very damaging to a portfolio.

Investment Institutions The largest investors in the stock market are generally referred to as "institutions." Often, they are companies, such as life insurance companies, who are in possession of funds that they are authorized to invest at their own discretion. The institution's funds are managed by professional "money managers" whose job it is to find the best possible place to invest the funds they manage.

Many investors who lack professional expertise in investing prefer to have their money managed by a person whose vocation it is to manage such funds. This has resulted in the advent of the *mutual fund*. Mutual funds are companies that take the money of many small investors and pool it so that they can act as a large investor and be managed by a professional money manager. Mutual funds grew rapidly in the United States during the 1960s, but in recent years their performance has not exceeded that of the average small investor, and the popularity of the conventional mutual fund has diminished. In their place have evolved more specialized funds such as money market funds. Money market funds invest in low-risk investment opportunities, such as large bank deposits which, because they are so large, yield higher returns than small investors could get on their own. Also, specialized funds have arisen that invest in particular commodities, such as commodity futures or gold and silver.

In recent years specialized mutual funds have appeared. These funds invest the money they manage in specific investment areas. Whereas mutual funds historically invested all their money in common stocks, these new funds allow small investors to have a professional money manager invest their funds in such opportunities as options or commodities.

Appendix: Answers to Self-Test Problems

CHAPTER 1

1. 3
2. 7
3. 64
4. -8.5
5. 56
6. -35
7. 2
8. 7
9. 11
10. 3
11. 1.5
12. 2.1

CHAPTER 2

1. $149.18
2. $8,588.16
3. 11.64 percent
4. 6.09 years
5. A is worth $211,683.47; B is worth $196,403.30. A is therefore better by $15,280.17.

CHAPTER 3

1. 91.22 months
2. 5.08 percent
3. $81,411.85
4. $1,733.09
5. $23,171.66
6. Annuity 1: NPV = $16,000; IRR = 13.94 percent
   Annuity 2: NPV = $23,000; IRR = 18.63 percent
   Bank: NPV = $8,621.66; IRR = 5.75 percent
   The best choice is Annuity 2 since both NPV and IRR are highest.
7. ABC: 7.04 percent
   XYZ: 4.91 percent
   ABC has the higher YTM.

CHAPTER 4

1. 6250 units
2. $3
3. 366,667 units

4. $500,000
5. (a) 42 units
   (b) 252 units

CHAPTER 6

1. (a) Net profit margin = 5.9 percent
   (b) Gross profit margin = 35.0 percent
   (c) Return on equity = 11.7 percent
   (d) Return on average equity = 12.5 percent
   (e) Return on total assets = 6.4 percent
   (f) Return on average assets = 7.0 percent
   (g) Debt to total assets ratio = 45.8 percent
   (h) Debt to equity ratio = 0.844:1
   (i) Long-term debt to total capitalization ratio = 40.6 percent
   (j) Current ratio = 12.9x
   (k) Quick ratio = 8.5x
   (l) Inventory turnover = 5.9x
   (m) Average inventory turnover = 8.1x
   (n) Accounts receivable turnover = 3.5x
   (o) Average accounts receivable turnover = 3.8x
   (p) Accounts receivable days = 96
   (q) Operating expense ratio = 65.0 percent
   (r) Interest coverage = 3.3x
2. Return on investment = 8.7 percent

CHAPTER 7

1.

Year	*Straight-Line*	*Double Declining Balance*	*Sum of the Years Digits*
1	$8,500	$18,333	$15,938
2	8,500	15,889	14,875
3	8,500	13,770	13,813
4	8,500	11,934	12,750
5	8,500	10,343	11,688
6	8,500	8,964	10,625
7	8,500	7,769	9,563
8	8,500	6,733	8,500
9	8,500	5,835	7,438
10	8,500	5,057	6,375

11	8,500	4,383	5,312
12	8,500	3,799	4,250
13	8,500	3,292	3,188
14	8,500	2,853	2,125
15	8,500	8,546	1,063

2.

Year	*Straight-Line*	*Double Declining Balance*	*Sum of the Years Digits*
1	$65,042	$133,000	$120,077
2	65,042	110,833	110,071
3	65,042	92,361	100,064
4	65,042	76,968	90,058
5	65,042	64,140	80,051
6	65,042	53,540	70,045
7	65,042	44,541	60,038
8	65,042	37,118	50,032
9	65,042	30,932	40,026
10	65,042	25,776	30,019
11	65,042	21,480	20,013
12	65,042	89,811	10,006

Index